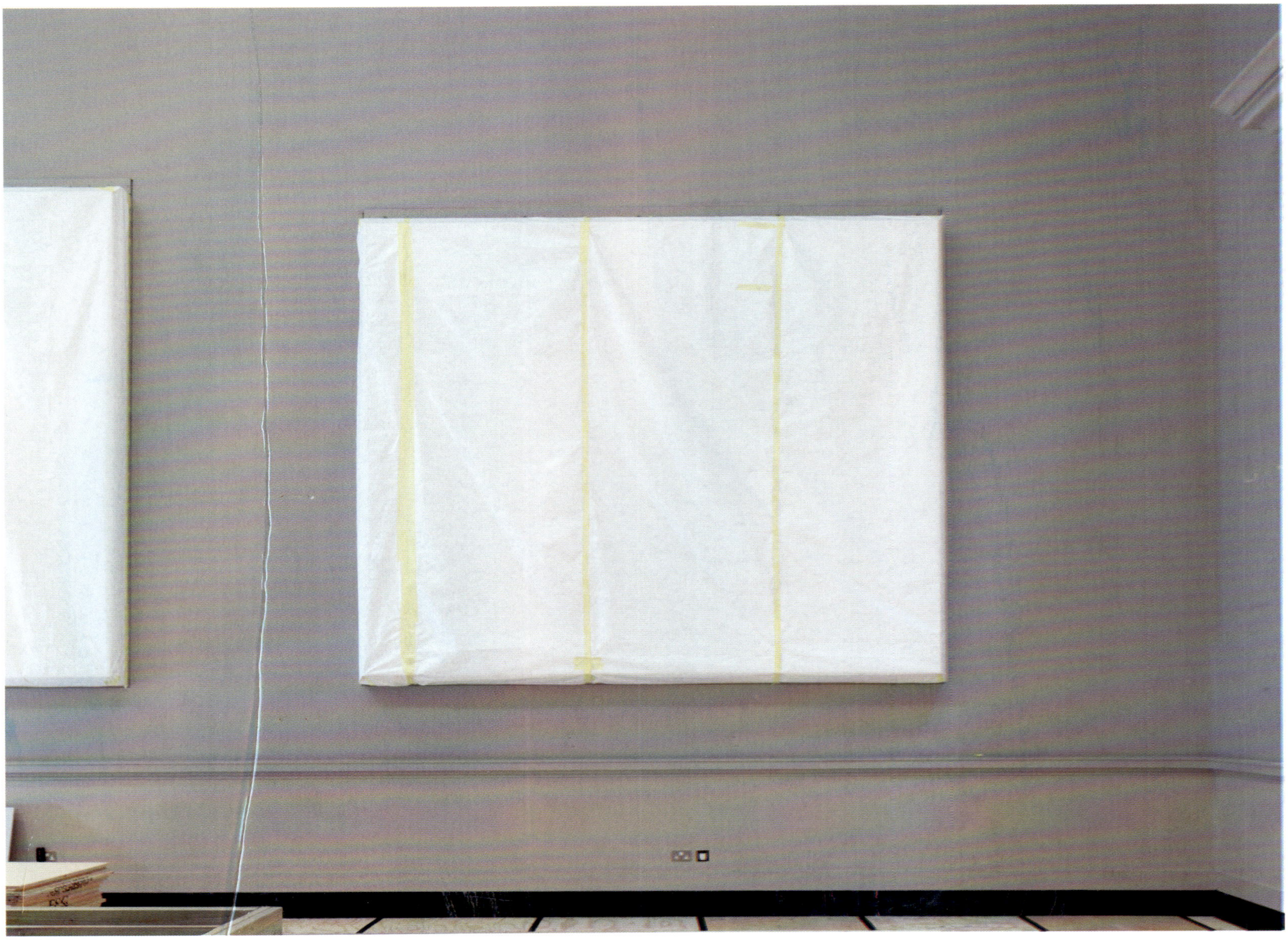

RAPHAEL VRB
IN
GEORGIVS MNT
VANVS
F.
ST PAUL IN THE SCHOOL OF ATHENS
ITALIAN SCHOOL.

THE RAPHAEL CARTOONS
1515-1516
The Acts of St Peter and St Paul
Lent by HER MAJESTY THE QUEEN

May 1865

Another view.

May 1865

Another view.

Raffaello Sanzio
Ritratto di gentildonna detto La muta

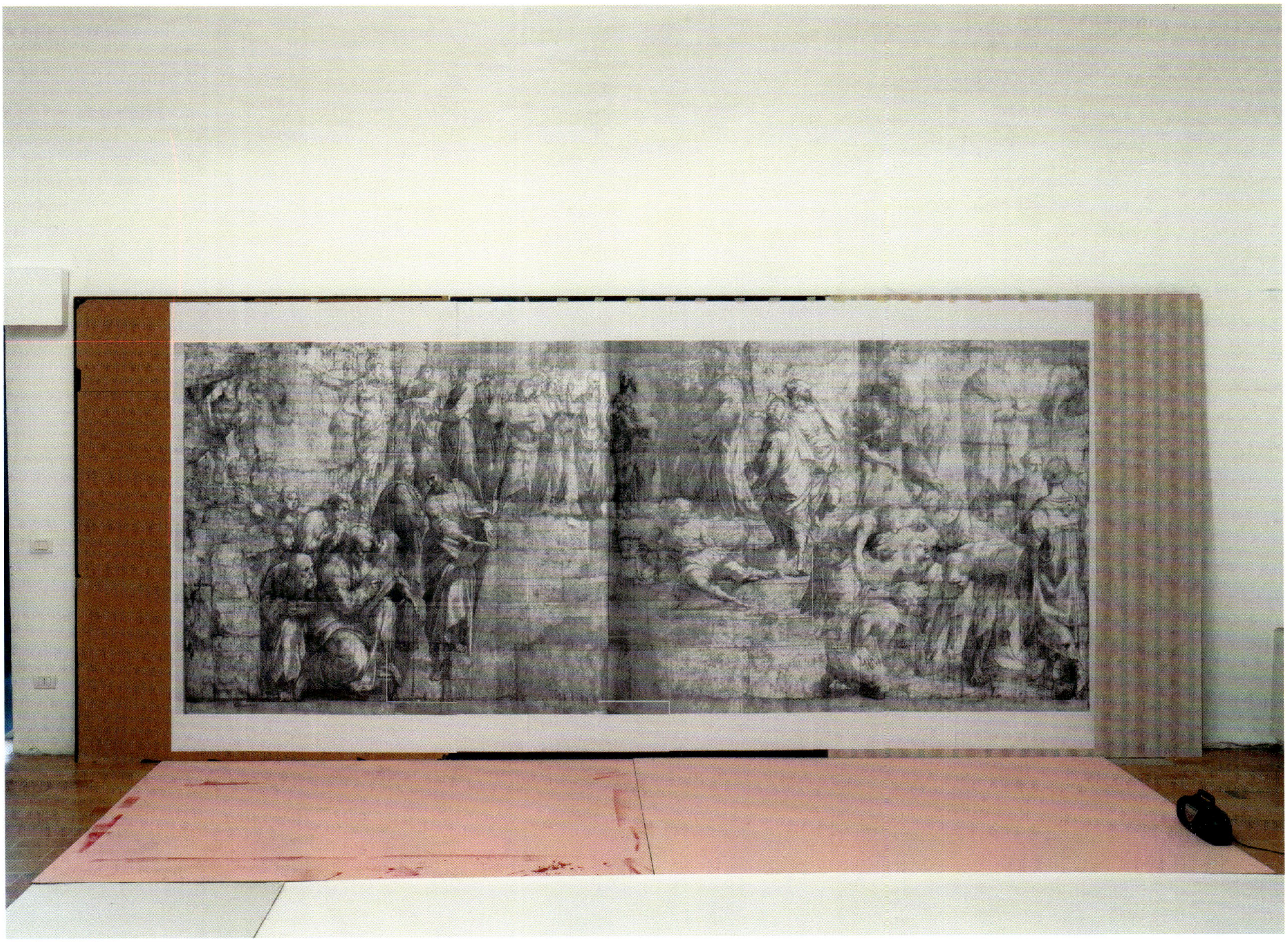

AVGVSTINO·CHISIO
SENENSI
VIRO·INLVSTRI
ATQVE·MAGNIFICO
SACELLI·HVIVS·FVNDATORI
QVI·OBIIT·AN·DOM·CIƆIƆXX

D·VIRGINI·LAVRETANAE·S·

Documents on Raphael
Stefano Graziani

Edited by Francesco Zanot

PALLADIO MUSEUM

Mousse Publishing

The Ghost Architect and His Hounds
Guido Beltramini

Superworks
Francesco Zanot

The Raphael Cartoons for the Sistine Chapel
in the Victoria and Albert Museum
Ana Debenedetti

Oblique Portraits
Ellis Woodman

Nothing Seems More Photographic
or Pictorial Than Love
Emanuele Coccia

Velvet Drapes
Pablo Bronstein

Hypothesis on the Clouds in the *School of Athens*
Pier Paolo Tamburelli

Raphael's Chigi Chapel: A Spatial Reading
Emanuel Christ

L'ossa con la carne, or Space Is Not Enough
Victoria Easton

Light from Above
Bruce Boucher

Grotesque
Manuel Orazi

Roman Architecture
Kersten Geers

A Letter to the Youth
Antonio Cataldo

In the Mind's Eye
Maddalena Scimemi

Raphael's Spatial Fantasies in the Garden
of Villa Madama
Frank Boehm

The Ghost Architect and His Hounds
Guido Beltramini

Five hundred and one years after its subject's birth, the 1984 *Raphael the Architect* exhibition at the Campidoglio in Rome was a laboratory from which a group of architecture historians emerged to impose a new vision of their discipline. At the helm stood Howard Burns, Christoph Frommel, Pier Nicola Pagliara, and Manfredo Tafuri. Their elder brethren Arnaldo Bruschi, Christof Thoenes, and above all James Ackerman, that last having led the way with his *The Cortile del Belvedere* (1954), were watching their backs.

Their postwar forefathers had communicated with the public through large monographs that—apart from Ackerman's masterpiece *The Architecture of Michelangelo* (1961)—constricted vision to black and white. This generation wanted the full range of grays. The exhibition was important because it was the public moment in which the history of architecture forever ceased being only a history of architectonic forms and typologies, intended for architects in an eternal disciplinary present. In a single stroke, it aged Bruno Zevi and Leonardo Benevolo, and also Vincent Scully.

The study of architecture of the past was brought into contexts; it became a humanistic discipline that intertwined ideologies, religion, economy, and mentalities on the basis of the material history of the *Annales* and Carlo Ginzburg's studies. At the center of this new history was the language of architecture, its stylistic features, its sources, its genealogies. And this language bore drawing with it. Certainly survey drawings, but no longer those of beaux-arts schools that record the shape of the building—rather, those that borrowed their techniques from archaeology to record the physical consistency of the building, its materials, and its construction phases, reading its evolution over time. Thus, a thicker wall could reveal a medieval preexistence that had conditioned the form of the building. A specific technique or material could be a clue toward a chronological interpretation of the parts, allowing for an understanding of the original creative idea.

But above all, Renaissance drawing was at the center, no longer seen as image but read as a tool with which the architect conceived and developed his own project, and then communicated it to his clients, skilled workers, and readers. This meant developing a new scholarship capable of reading architectural drawings—their autography, their materiality. The study drawings became more interesting than the presentation drawings, because the former record interrupted tracks. It was necessary to recognize the watermarks in order to date the drawings. Autography and erasures became important, as did the types of media, from ink to black chalk to red chalk.

Interest in drawing was complemented by new attention to the reconstruction of unbuilt projects so as to make history not solely out of the winners—that is, the built buildings. Through drawings, the discovery of unbuilt works marked a fundamental shift, as it meant centering the architect's creative personality rather than his built works, considering that in architecture—unlike sculpture or painting—unbuilt projects often bear innovative features. The 1984 exhibition, so centered on drawing, could only have occurred at a time when, among practicing architects, postmodernism was once again placing drawing at the center of contemporary architecture, using it as a privileged field of research (as with Aldo Rossi) and collecting and exhibiting it (the Deutsches Architekturmuseum opened in Frankfurt in 1984).

The 1984 exhibition gave substance to a ghost, Raphael the architect, who had played a key role in the invention of Renaissance architecture. Raphael added flesh and skin to the bone structure of the orders developed by Donato Bramante, reinventing the surfaces of buildings according to Roman ruins. His buildings mirrored his clients' personalities, made them distinguishable on the urban scene as actors on a stage. He organized a systematic archaeological survey campaign of ancient ruins. He theoretically defined the methods of architectural drawing in terms of plans, elevations, and sections, as opposed to the representations of painters. In the studies of the facade of Saint Peter's, for the first time a giant and a minor order interweave, but it would take thirty years, and Michelangelo and Andrea Palladio, to see them in the real world. With Villa Madama, he reinvented the country residence, giving form to a tradition that dated back to the ancient Romans. Yet even this tremendous contribution has almost been erased from history. Palazzo Branconio dell'Aquila was demolished; Palazzo Jacopo da Brescia was dismantled and reassembled in a different site; the church of Sant'Eligio degli Orefici was altered; Villa Madama is a wonderful but incomplete fragment; the Chigi stables today lie in ruins; and the plan for Saint Peter's survives only in the pages of the Codex Mellon in New York.

Shortly before his death, Tafuri was asked what he thought was the most beautiful house in the world. He answered: "A house that has never been built—the house Raphael designed for himself in Via Giulia."

Superworks
Francesco Zanot

If photography had been available, Raphael most probably would have used it, first and foremost to carry out his study on ancient monuments. The artist from Urbino was well known for his excellence not only in the fields of painting and architecture, but also in that of archaeology. So much so as to have been assigned the study of the Roman legacy by Pope Leo X, founding a good part of the prestige that he enjoyed in the papal court on "his fame as a significant connoisseur of classical antiquity."[1] Having neither film nor lenses at his disposal, Raphael entrusted to technical drawing the task of recording traces of the past, organizing genuine survey campaigns that rhyme with the documentary frenzy of the decades following the birth of photography. A few centuries later, we would speak of agencies and correspondents to describe the extraordinary organizational effort Vitruvius attributed to the Rafaelesque institution: "Such was his *greatness* that he kept draftsmen all over *Italy*, in *Pozzuoli*, *and* even in Greece and he was searching out everything of the good that might help his art."[2]

1 Christoph L. Frommel, "Raffaello e la sua carriera architettonica," in *Raffaello architetto*, ed. Christoph L. Frommel, Stefano Ray, and Manfredo Tafuri (Milan: Electa, 1984), 45.

2 Giorgio Vasari, "Vita di Raffaello d'Urbino pittore et architetto," in *Le vite de' più eccellenti pittori, scultori e architettori* (Florence: Sansoni, 1906), 663.

The photographic work carried out by Stefano Graziani in 2020 originates precisely from this intuition. It sinks its roots into the same middle ground upon which Raphael's very own program rested: not solely scholar of the past, but contemporaneously inventor of the future. Appointed to the post of commissioner of antiquities on August 27, 1515, with the precise aim of preventing the destruction of most epigraphic marble blocks, Raphael imagined a sequence of actions that went beyond protection, involving projects related to cataloguing, conservation, and, most of all, reconstruction. Moreover, he took advantage of this historical knowledge, acquired in tandem with his creative work, to then include it in his own artistic production. Among the most famous examples is the archway to the Chigi Chapel (an evident reference to the portal of the Pantheon) and the decoration of Villa Madama (inspired by some of the motifs of the Domus Aurea). Five hundred years later, Graziani intervenes in this dialogue, reactivating it. His photographs only apparently reproduce parts of the Raphaelesque oeuvre; more precisely, they are images of their relationship with the present.

"Can you see the moon can you see it seen," wrote Gertrude Stein a century ago in a sentence that directly indicated an aspect, as revolutionary as it was inevitable, of the very nature of photography.[3] What one can see through this tool, in fact, is not the subject itself (the moon, which we observe by raising our eyes to the sky), but its image filtered through the gaze of someone who has seen it for us. If this is valid for any photograph, in the case of Graziani's work it is also a fundamental object of study. Presenting a series of artworks dealing with the thought of an essential genius of the

Italian Renaissance, Graziani measures our distance from them. We are in the vast field of transformation.

Carlo Mollino, an architect with a visceral attachment to photography, would have used the term "transfiguration," highlighting the mystic vein of a process that still has very concrete roots.[4] In fact, in Graziani's images we recognize works that, in reality, are very different. Paintings, tapestries, architecture—they have all become photographs. It is the cornerstone of the vitality of this medium, which instead of "immortalizing" its very subject revives it, revealing an always new perspective. Anything but inert, Graziani's works offer the pleasure of the surprise of discovering something that has already been discovered. It is a question of circularity (see Gertrude Stein): they are works about works. In short, they hyperbolize a criterion already used by Raphael and already mentioned above, namely the quote. If photography has often been considered a form of appropriation, emphasizing its unilateral and predatory characteristics, here Graziani substantially shifts this paradigm: the source is known. Beyond offering itself to a new interpretation, the subject functions as a means to illuminate what surrounds it, within and out of the frame.

3 Gertrude Stein, "A Circular Play" (1920), in *A Stein Reader*, ed. Ulla E. Dydo (Evanston, IL: Northwestern University Press, 1993), 326–42.

4 See Carlo Mollino, "I mezzi tecnico-fotografici di trasfigurazione estetica della natura," in *Il messaggio dalla camera oscura* (Turin: Chiantore, 1949), 71. Unless otherwise noted, original texts are rendered in English by the translator.

Investigating the transformative ability of photography, Graziani highlights the altered nature of his subjects. In practice, none of them correspond to the work that appeared to Raphael's eyes, yet in any case we are dealing with the result of different events and modifications occurring over the course of time. From restorations, renovations, and reconstructions to *ex novo* realizations based on original plans, these projects indicate the distance between past and present. The system the artist from Urbino had already considered during his scientific assignment at the Vatican reenters the scene. Graziani represents its great expansion in the contemporary period, made of places (museums, universities, archives), things (diagnostic technologies, innovative materials, displays), and people (directors, conservators, registrars). It is a mammoth and refined device developed to defend an economic and cultural patrimony.

Questions of power overlie ethical imperatives, dictating the safeguarding of what we still have in order to pass it on to future generations, even with the awareness of a limit to the possibilities of maintaining and replicating this chain. Realism clashes with utopia, reawakening an aspiration—that of slowing down or stopping time, which crosses the entire history of human speculation, from Penelope's shroud to Marvel superheroes. Centuries before Marcel Duchamp and Joseph Kosuth, Raphael appears here in the guise of the conceptual artist whose idea outweighs its realization. In an operation both similar and contrary to that carried out by Walter Benjamin on the corpus of photography, Graziani questions the aura of the works he is faced with and examines the relationship they entertain with the spectator.

Perhaps some brushstrokes on the surface of a fresco were not produced by the hand of Raphael, but rather by the expertise of a technician busy regenerating colors like a Photoshop algorithm. Perhaps Raphael never rested his back on the very wall that today supports the building. Graziani demolishes certainties to generate questions. He takes up the theme of the relationship between original and copy so dear to art history (at least since the very act of collecting instigated the multiplication of reproductions during the Hellenistic period) and that of photography. Only here, original and copy would be the same. Individual works would become the product of an enormous structure. Superworks. Nonetheless perishable and extremely delicate. Graziani's narration oscillates frighteningly between strength and fragility. Thus, instead of dedicating single images to some of the subjects, he makes brief series composed of photographs that are slightly different from one another, with an almost cinematographic pace, recalling the horizontal continuity of the Raphaelesque oeuvre. Comparing them, what remains (resists) emerges together with all that vanishes. Two opposing terms here appear so extraordinarily similar.

The Raphael Cartoons for the Sistine Chapel in the Victoria and Albert Museum
Ana Debenedetti

To mark the five hundredth anniversary of Raphael's death in 2020, the Victoria and Albert Museum (V&A) in London has embarked on a major renovation project of the so-called Raphael Court (gallery 48A), current home of the seven surviving cartoons for tapestries that Raphael designed in about 1515–16 for the Sistine Chapel at the Vatican, Rome. The status, meaning, and visibility of the cartoons have gone through various phases of presentation and interpretation over the years. The new presentation will enhance in an unprecedented way how we look at these monumental works, allowing us to understand them as unique Renaissance treasures, both in terms of aesthetic value and technical achievement. The cartoons depict key episodes from the lives of Saint Peter and Saint Paul, and each of them is composed of nearly two hundred sheets of paper, each measuring around 42 or 43 centimeters in height by 28.5 or 29 centimeters in width. During the summer of 2019, the V&A conducted a new program of photography using the pioneering technique of three-dimensional scanning combined with other types of imaging, such as infrared reflectography. To enable this, the glazing was removed from the cartoons allowing curators and conservators to observe closely not only the impressive texture of these five-hundred-year-old works on paper, akin to elephant skin with its roughened areas, creases, and tears, but also Raphael's supremely versatile ingenuity. His power of invention allowed him to not only conform to the style of the preexisting decoration of the chapel but also conceive a series whose narrative would clearly relate to the scenes depicted above the lower register where the tapestries were to be hung.

On this occasion, the cartoons also revealed their true and exceptionally fresh colors. Raphael employed a cool, acidic palette in order to link his compositions chromatically with the earlier frescoes. Pietro Perugino, Sandro Botticelli, Domenico Ghirlandaio, and Luca Signorelli, among others, completed the first phase of the decorative program with scenes of the lives of Christ and Moses for Pope Sixtus IV (Francesco della Rovere, r. 1471–84) in 1483. A further challenge was for Raphael to harmonize his designs with Michelangelo's recent fresco ceiling depicting scenes from the Book of Genesis with figures of the sibyls and prophets (1508–12). The altar wall, on the other hand, still retained the frescoed altarpiece of the Assumption by Perugino, flanked by two narrative scenes, which would be later covered by Michelangelo's *Last Judgment* (1536–41). Rediscovering the true colors of the cartoons brought the compositions to life; all the figures seemed suddenly engaged in swirling gestures, interacting with each other, while the whole series appeared to be breathing, moving, reacting as a whole ensemble despite being incomplete (three cartoons are still lost). Only then, one could understand the true role and status of these large designs, stylistically conceived as a structural basis (*basamento*) for the scenes depicted above. With their large figures, solidly settled in the foreground, and their clear narrative, the resulting tapestries would draw the eye to the upper level in a play of chromatic harmony.

Created at a formidable pace by Raphael and his team for a medium—tapestry—that he had never previously worked for, the cartoons were immediately sent abroad to be woven in the workshop of the Brussels merchant-weaver Pieter van Aelst (1450–1533). From then on, they disappeared from public sight for nearly a century: duplicates were produced to be used on the looms, as the weaving process would have considerably damaged Raphael's masterpieces. For the first time, a series of tapestries, which were traditionally conceived as movable luxury goods and had the flexibility to be arranged differently each time according to the venue, had been created for a specific site. The use of perspective, and the drama and arrangement of Raphael's designs, took the genre in an entirely new direction. It is generally believed that the tapestries were originally made for a particular hanging arrangement within the Sistine Chapel given their various dimensions, specific light sources (which respectively alternate from left to right), and sequential narrative order. What this original sequence might have been continues to the subject of debate, but Raphael probably saw and might even have supervised the first display of the tapestries when seven of them were delivered to the Vatican in time for the mass of St. Stephen in 1519. His premature death in April 1520 prevented him to see the complete set. The remaining three reached the Vatican by December 1521, just before the pope died. The death of their creator followed by that of the commissioner had probably no little bearing on the fate of the cartoons themselves, which were presumed lost for nearly a century until seven of them reappeared in Genoa in the early seventeenth century. However, as early as 1521, one of them, the *Conversion of Saul* (now lost), found its way back to Italy, as it was recorded in the important collection of Cardinal Grimani in Venice (1461–1523).

From the beginning of the sixteenth century, highly finished (*ben finito*), generally monochrome, cartoons were increasingly being produced as preparatory designs for frescoes and easel paintings: some were subsequently presented to important patrons. This development coincided with a new taste for collecting works on paper on the Italian peninsula and beyond. It is therefore likely that all were intended to enter prestigious collections, or to be returned to the pope so that he could keep control of their reproduction or employ them as gifts; he could also, if necessary, hang them as substitutes for the finished tapestries, as was the practice in some northern European churches. Instead, tradition has it that Peter Paul Rubens discovered them in the early 1600s in Genoa and later alerted the Prince of Wales, future King Charles I (r. 1625–49), to their existence. The cartoons were specifically acquired in 1623 by the English Crown as designs for the recently founded tapestry manufactory in Mortlake (west of London). There, new duplicates were created while the cartoons themselves were put back into storage for another eighty years. It was only under the reign of William III (r. 1682–1702) that the cartoons regained their status as works of art in their own right. A gallery was specifically designed in Hampton Court Palace for their display, making them the only monumental works by Raphael available outside Italy. The cartoons were progressively praised as national treasures and played a significant role in the rise of an art historical awareness in Britain. With the accession of Queen Victoria in 1837 and the subsequent opening of Hampton Court Palace to the public, the cartoons become increasingly accessible, and by the mid-nineteenth century entered a new phase of their history by being associated with an ambitious enterprise known as the Raphael Collection, devised by Albert, prince consort to the queen (1819–61). The collection included more than 5,000 prints and photographs after every work regarded at this time as being by, or after, Raphael in order to provide a unique visual resource in the study of the master. The prince consort's premature death in December 1861 prevented him from seeing the completion of his project. It was therefore as a tribute to his memory that the queen agreed in 1865 to lend the cartoons to the recently founded South Kensington Museum (now the V&A), whose cultural and educational agenda had been partly devised by the prince.

Contemplating, observing, and exploring the Raphael cartoons today allows us to reconcile their role as functional designs and their status as absolute masterpieces, indissolubly linked to Raphael's creative process. Made for a specific site and purpose, Raphael's vast "woven frescoes" set an example of a true revolution in design which, we hope, will continue to inspire future generations.

Oblique Portraits
Ellis Woodman

Among the holdings of London's Victoria and Albert Museum (V&A) is a set of plate-glass negatives, each of which is an epically dimensioned 3 feet square and 1/4 of an inch thick. They were produced in 1858 by the institution's first in-house photographer, Charles Thurston Thompson, and record the cycle of seven Raphael cartoons that were then housed at Hampton Court Palace on the capital's western outskirts. On average, each cartoon is 5 meters long and 3.5 meters high, which made it impossible to photograph them in the gallery where they had been installed. On days of fine weather, they were therefore lowered out of a window and into an adjacent courtyard, allowing Thompson to photograph them in daylight with the aid of a camera of unknown but presumably monumental size. From the negatives, albumen prints were made, which conservators annotated to provide an exacting record of the cartoons' physical condition. The exercise represented one of the earliest and most ambitious uses of photography to document a work of art.

As Walter Benjamin famously argued in his 1935 essay "The Work of Art in the Age of Mechanical Reproduction," the advent of photography dramatically diminished the sense of authority or "aura" that a work of art had historically projected. And yet, the fact that the cartoons were among the first images to undergo such a jeopardizing multiplication is not without irony. These were, after all, never conceived as definitive works of art in their own right but as design documents that would enable the production of tapestries by other hands. Employing many sheets of paper glued together on a canvas backing, Raphael and his studio produced the cartoons, which depict scenes from the Gospels and the Acts of the Apostles, between 1515 and 1516. They were then sent to Brussels, where the studio of Pieter van Aelst spent three years weaving, enabling the tapestries' first presentation in the Sistine Chapel on St. Stephen 1519.

In fact, these were only the first of a series of versions produced from the cartoons; both King Henry VIII of England and Francis I of France acquired sets. Meanwhile, as early as 1516, the cartoons had also been employed as the basis for the production of prints and proved particularly well suited to reinterpretation in this medium as Raphael, knowing that his designs would have to work effectively as tapestries, had concentrated on bold compositional effects rather than intricate detail. It was primarily through the proliferation of prints that Raphael's designs established a central place in the European cultural imagination.

But by the time Charles Thurston Thompson came to make his photographic representations of the cartoons, the smoothly idealized and eminently reproducible nature of Raphael's images had begun to attract significant criticism. When John Ruskin first visited Rome in 1840, he recorded: "Of Raphael, however, I found I could make nothing whatever. The only thing clearly manifest to me in his compositions was that everybody seemed to be pointing at everybody else, and that nobody, to my notion, was worth pointing at." The frescoes of 1509–11 in the Stanza della Segnatura in the Vatican proved a source of particular vexation for the English critic. "And from that spot, and from that hour," Ruskin wrote, "the intellect and the art of Italy date their degradation. [. . .] And it was brought about in great part by the very excellencies of the man who had thus marked the commencement of the decline. The perfection of execution and the beauty of feature which were attained in these works and in those of his greatest contemporaries, rendered finish of execution and beauty of form the chief objects of all artists; and henceforward execution was looked for rather than thought, and beauty rather than veracity."[1]

1 *The Works of John Ruskin*, ed. E. T. Cook, Alexander Wedderburn (Library Edition) (London: George Allen 1903-12), Vol. 12, 148.

Ruskin's belief that Raphael's achievements represented an ossification of the more vital tendencies of medieval art ran counter to the view of Britain's Royal Academy of Arts, which was strongly promoting the Italian master as a model for a resurgence of contemporary history painting. The cartoons, which were on public display at Hampton Court, formed a central plank of that campaign. But Ruskin's criticisms of Raphael resonated strongly with a younger generation of British artists. In 1848, a group which included William Holman Hunt, John Everett Millais, and Dante Gabriel Rossetti established the Pre-Raphaelite Brotherhood with the express purpose of reconnecting contemporary art to a tradition that they believed Raphael had corrupted. The close observation of nature, and its representation in abundant detail, became a central principle of the Brotherhood's war against academicism.

In 1865 Thompson made a further set of photographs that can be found in the V&A's collection, this time recording a six-meter-high, horse-drawn packing case into which the cartoons were soon to be installed. Queen Victoria had recently agreed to place the cartoons on long-term loan to the new museum which had been named in her and her husband's honor, and the bespoke case had been commissioned with the purpose of transporting them from Hampton Court. It was the elaborate technical infrastructure required to ensure the preservation of these most fragile objects that held the photographer's attention. Paradoxically, the decision not to present the cartoons explicitly communicates a greater sense of their physical presence. Thompson's oblique portraits reawaken the aura that their long history of reproduction has done so much to dim.

Nothing Seems More Photographic or Pictorial than Love
Emanuele Coccia

Nothing seems more photographic or pictorial than love. No other feeling seems so connected to vision; no other relationship seems to nourish itself with light, form, colors. Conversely, it is precisely because of this intimacy with forms and vision that love seems to be obsessively visited by the arts that feed themselves on images, and thus so connected to their history. If it is not possible to love without being able to imagine—to immerse oneself in the visual image of the other—then every act of imagination is an exercise of love. This is why one of the medieval treatises—Andrea Cappellano's *De Amore*—that so influenced European literature and culture for centuries defined love as "a certain innate passion that proceeds from vision and the excessive consideration of the form of the other kind, for which someone desires above all else to possess the embraces of the other and, through shared will, the commandments of love can be realized in these embraces." These lines condense the experience of modern love and the poetics of European modernity.

The connection between vision and love is so deep that it is almost impossible for us to recognize its contingency. Love has not always been a passion born from vision. In the version Apuleius provided in his *Metamorphoses*, the story of Cupid and Psyche is a treatise on love insofar as it is a relationship and a passion *not* accessible through images and vision. This strange form of iconoclasm gives rhythm to and structures the myth. It is because her beauty is too apparent that Psyche cannot find love; one observes her as one observes art ("*mirantur quidem divinam speciem sed ut simulacrum fabre politum mirantur omnes*"). Once united with Cupid, she disappears from the sight of all other men. But it is in the relationship that the absence of vision becomes decisive. In fact, the *forma mariti* is not accessible, and any form of desire for vision is branded as sacrilegious curiosity. The union occurs *praeter oculos*—only through touch and sound. Here we are dealing not only with a prohibition, but with an impossibility. Once the face of Cupid has been seen, he will be forced to forever elude the sight of his beloved. "You will never see again if you have seen," Cupid warns Psyche. Psyche's love is constructed as an act of resistance to the denied image ("*denegatae sacrosanctae imaginis tuae*"), a devotion to one who has no face, or the ability to do without one ("*nec quicquam amplius in tuo vultu requiro*"). And finally, Psyche's last mission, aimed to win the favor of Venus, bore a ban on viewing the contents of a box ("*hoc observandum praecipue tibi censeo e velis aperire vel inspicere illam quam feres pyxidem vel omnino divinae dormonsitatis abditum curiosus temptare thesaurum*").

The heart of the tale lies in this paradox: the relationship with the god Cupid (*deus totius ignis*, god of all fire, and therefore of light) presupposes the escape from all light, or to say it in Apuleius's words, it is a "lucifugous" relationship that is horrified by light. Thanks to this "aniconic" nature, love can be assimilated to a mystery, in the religious and cultic sense of the term.

As such, Apuleius's tale has nothing "mythological" about it. On the contrary, it seems to translate and, through narration, elucidate an experience of love that is much more familiar and daily than what it identified as an undisciplined exercise of sight. In this sphere of existence, loving always means entering into a religious, liturgical relationship with the other. Rhythmic and regular association and the sharing of spaces and times do not take place in the cognitive sphere and are not aimed at getting to know the other. Love is nourished by contact and seeks intimacy, not knowledge and identity. Love is the possibility of closeness to someone whose name and face continue to elude us. It is an exercise in willing and faithful blindness to whom we can speak and touch but will never be able to see.

Painting this erotic experience, as Raphael's cycle of frescoes in the Loggia of Cupid and Psyche attempts, means clashing with an impossibility. How can one paint the negation of the image of the other?

If Raphael tried to have it out with his own limits through painting, Stefano Graziani's attempt to photograph the cycle is even more vertiginous. It is not just a question of transforming a pictorial work into a photographic vision that must stage a tactile and auditory, rather than a visual and optical, love. It is about inscribing the very relationship between photography and painting in the sphere of aniconic love. Photography no longer must reproduce pictorial vision. No longer is there a competition about knowing reality better; no longer is there the attempt to reproduce the pictorial exercise to the highest degree of fidelity. The paintings are barely visible. What is staged is only intimacy, a proximity with the pictorial image that seems inaccessible, just like the face of Cupid. The photographic series focuses on the loggia, on its atmosphere, as if to suggest the presence of the observer in that space, rather than accurately repeating the visual experience of Raphael's work. It is not so much the image or the sense of the work of Raphael, nor the meaning of his art, that is transformed, but the relationship between the photographic medium and reality. Faced with a tradition that makes photography a form of *immoderata cogitatio* of reality—an outdated and completely visual imagination—these photographs seem to want to update Apuleius's program of love without image.

In Graziani's work, photography becomes this loving exercise of faithful and religious blindness to reality. It does not aim to discover its face nor fix its identity. It does not arouse love for things, places, people, illuminating their features. It is something closer to a nocturnal encounter with someone or something whose name and origin are unknown. The camera is a mechanical, repeated, liturgical cult for the bodies with which we continue to clash. It is a way to promise them that we no longer need their faces. Photography becomes a mystery—a way to ensure, on a daily basis, that we can know the world, literally, even without our eyes.

Velvet Drapes
Pablo Bronstein

Languid young men drape over velvet stools. Some delicately rest thin hands on gilt sword hilts that will never unsheathe. Others hold up small roundels of their beloveds while staring vaguely at the viewer as if to say, "You go and work the fields—I'm busy." Although there was a historicist revival of chivalry in fifteenth- and sixteenth-century Europe, demonstrated through the popularity of Ariosto and the countless paintings of Saint George slaying the dragon, gallantry at court often needed working on. In 1528 Baldassarre Castiglione (of whom Raphael painted a portrait) published *Il Cortegiano*, or *The Book of the Courtier*. Set as an informal semipublic conversation at the court of Urbino in 1507, Castiglione instructs the budding courtier in manners and comportment. Ducal courts were social spaces where people often ate, shat, and slept together in large rooms. How well you opened a door for a lady could be the difference between pleasing or annoying someone in a position to help or hinder your rise. The book aims to ensure that the courtier is up to speed, not on manners as a set of rules, but as a personal grace with which to dazzle the prince whom one serves. The emphasis is on a relaxed style of bearing, creating an aura of natural superiority, a physical "elegance" born of an open and easy disposition, on lithe, gentle movements, and an aristocratic countenance. This effortless, high-class charm was coined *sprezzatura*.

Smoothing over the edges and awkward angles of an unruly "natural" body, *sprezzatura* is like a uniform that hides behavioral irregularities, tidying up the individual. Individuality is, of course, not always desirable, especially if a courtier seeks to blend in and make it appear that he belongs. As the desired attitude is of friendly aloofness, this code permits inner intentions to go unnoticed, much like a ballet dancer hides the physical effort of a leap with a graceful curvature of the spine. *Sprezzatura* is therefore not only a uniform, but a mask. According to the book, the courtier should mask effort, and in so doing, mask ambition: "Why would I bother to plot against you when I barely know who you are?" In the age of Raphael and Castiglione the *sprezzatura* performer is a *professional* courtier, a socially aspirant agent of his own success, occupying a recognisably modern in-between space between merchant, peasant, and prince.

Who are these superior beings populating Raphael's religious and philosophical scenes? They are an ideal type, and the book of the courtier strives to instill that ideal in the reader. Yet the best way of communicating *sprezzatura* is not through books, but through paintings. Painting is large, in color, and sits in important rooms throughout the city. Hence, its use in communicating gesture and pose was paramount, comparable to film's role in influencing speech. By looking at paintings, people could see what "good" gestures were. Gestures associated with divinity and power (Michelangelo's hand of God creating Adam), with virtue and intelligence (Raphael's *School of Athens*), with sophistication and charm (the hands of Leonardo's *Mona Lisa*). Furthermore, it was only in Raphael's generation that physical elegance was rendered convincingly. The Venuses and Virgins of Botticelli or Signorelli might have had elegant leanings, but their fingers had not yet rid themselves of late-medieval boniness. Painting provides the fixed point of the pose—the position at which one must arrive. With this template there is no room for interpretation, unlike, say, having to interpret the word "refined" in *Il Cortegiano*.

It would be amusing to imagine that painting influenced people to move about occasionally striking "famous" poses. Between holding their hands like Adam and holding them like the Mona Lisa, might they revert back to a pre-elegant "natural" state? Or perhaps they managed to blend their movements into a lava flow of *sprezzatura*. Does Raphael paint the perfect moment, or perfect people? To hold one's head at a fetching angle can be copied from a portrait, and no doubt every clumsy Renaissance lump was able to pull that one out of the bag. But how does one tie one's shoelace with *sprezzatura*? How open a door for a lady? If you lift your arm to hold your wrist in a particular position, relaxing your fingers into a charming array around the door handle, what happens to the hand when you suddenly have to move the elbow and pull? How would the bumpkin not tie himself up into the most ridiculous knots? What if while concentrating on your elegant arms, you don't notice that your feet are turned inward and your knees touch as you walk? Thinking ahead physically in terms of the whole body is something dancers and mimes, experts in improvisation, are capable of, but laypeople find difficult to do. Indeed, comic literature is full of courtiers and pages tripping over their own feet.

The serene stares of those eyelashed youths speak of a glamorous, melancholic inner ease they were born with, and an exterior that is merely a reflection of inner harmony. But can *sprezzatura* percolate its way from the outside in? If you follow the instructions in the book and dangle your left leg limply over your right, do violent thoughts give way to a better temper? And if so, is everyone in *sprezzatura* feeling the same thing? Do they "become" the same "person," similar to the way the Victorian gentleman's bowler hat communicated both his conventional role within society as well as his conventional, "decent" inner life? Raphael's figures look relaxed indeed, inside and out, but as the sixteenth century progressed, *sprezzatura* was increasingly used by artists to evoke difficult emotional states. Artists such as Pontormo, Parmigianino, and Rosso Fiorentino distorted the body beyond plausibility in order to create a sort of emotional hyperbole. Ridiculously long legs, torsos twisting 180 degrees with ease, creepily over-articulated fingers, giraffe necks veering off into space—these bodies not only communicate supreme superhuman elegance, but also imbue the pictures with a complicated inner tension. Going against Raphael's Classicism, these stretched, elegantised bodies invoke a camp hysteria.

Castiglione is worried about an over-mannered effeminacy in some courtiers. Aimed at an ideal comportment, there is clearly a need to correct it in both directions. There are either boorish provincial thugs eating with their hands, or men that have become a little too interested in each other's company, too aware of their charms, and have over-softened. The presumably favored middle ground implies that the dubious fag in the painting will never pick up armour and defend the fair lady, and likewise the mercenary boor will never make her swoon with the strum of the lute under the arbor. Though in actual fact, many of these floppy, melting figures that grace the Mannerist portraits, for whom lifting a single hand of Christ during the descent from the Cross would already be too much of an effort, were in reality psychopathically violent.

In Raphael's paintings these figures are a perfectly balanced equation of elegance and composure. His *contrapposto* men seem lively rather than bored, gentle but not limp, touching the ground lightly rather than pirouetting through space. But *sprezzatura* in painting is a language of in-between gestures and non-definitive states. Though poses in *sprezzatura* can become codified, they are not definitive of anything but themselves. It is a hand that may be pointing, but not with urgency. It might be lifting a sword, but we know it won't use it. At court, *sprezzatura* must have been a language of sitting around and chatting, and therefore meaningless to those who had to work with their hands. The focus on hands in *sprezzatura* implies ones that neither till soil nor scrub clothes. But the reverse is also true: that elegance can *only* be achieved if you do not have to do these things, or if work *is* socializing, and manual labour an abstraction. Courts that approach maximum levels of languid delicacy, where *sprezzatura* reigns most supremely, are "decadent." The court of Versailles, the court of Charles I, the court of the Romanovs—these courts are stale, paralysed, and solely focused on inner intrigue and hair. These courts love ballet and tassels, makeup and gossip, and, of course, are full of queens.

Hypothesis on the Clouds in the *School of Athens*

Pier Paolo Tamburelli

Vasari wrote that Bramante "taught many of the rules of architecture to Raffaello da Urbino; designing for him, for example, the buildings that Raffaello afterwards drew in perspective in that apartment of the Pope wherein there is Mount Parnassus; in which apartment he made a portrait of Bramante taking measurements with a pair of compasses."[1]

1 Giorgio Vasari, *Le vite de' più eccellenti pittori, scultori e architettori; con nuove annotazioni e commenti di Gaetano Milanesi. Tomo IV* (Florence: Sansoni, 1878), 159.

I see no reason to doubt this extremely detailed testimony. What is more, it does not tell that Bramante himself had drawn the scene we now call the *School of Athens* and had given it to Raphael already completed. By that time (1509?), Bramante, old and with hands affected by tremors, could not work as before. In all probability, he no longer could draw. It is more credible that Bramante, once again curator of the Roman art scene of the early sixteenth century, simply suggested to Raphael how to face the problem. And certainly some of the features of the *spectacle of space* through which the philosophers walk and debate is Bramantesque: the walls are bare, without too much adornment; the building is made of a uniform material; the sequence of large, barrel-vaulted, coffered naves, the walls rhythmed with small inward variations, produces a perspective that progressively narrows, almost as if measuring the time necessary to cross it. The two vaults closest to the spectator are separated by a higher space, which, judging by its luminosity, is intended to be an open-air courtyard rather than sealed by a dome, as is traditionally believed to have been a principle for any Renaissance building.

The "building" produced by the scene of the *School of Athens* is a painted one and should be understood as such—as a series of parallel scenes, with no architectural requirements, at times even rather incoherent, almost too full of light, without any covering structure if not for the half-tubes of the barrel vaults that perpendicularly connect the various planes of the picture. This "building" is completely at the service of the painting and systematically sacrifices its architectural coherence for its visual clarity as painting, evident in the deliberately wrong detail of the non-inclined cornices of the non-diagonal pilasters upon which should sit the "dome" that we do not see. Thus far, these are all games, tricks, and manias of Bramante. But what does Raphael add?

Raphael paints the clouds. The scenes of the *School of Athens* leave three portions of the sky available for their placement. Starting from above: a window with two columns at the level of the drum of the (non)dome, a lunette caught between the lower margin of the second barrel vault and the Doric frieze that closes the arch on the backdrop, and the passage at the center of the arch over the heads of Aristotle and Plato. The sky becomes clearer as it proceeds downward, moving from an intense azure where the clouds distinctly stand out to an increasingly pale blue where sky and clouds blend. Counting the clouds, always from top to bottom, a frayed and bluish veil is seen on the right, in the great window of the drum; a large and compact white cumulus appears on the left in the drum window above and below the vault; another, softer cumulus appears on the right, cut by the frieze with triglyphs of the arch; and finally, above the heads of Plato and Aristotle are lighter layers (stratocumulus?) that fade into the whiteness of the distant sky. The main element is the great ball of vapor appearing in the window above and below the vault, a single mass transported by the wind (definitely from left to right, though I cannot explain why) toward the center of the image.

The importance of the cloudscape in the *School of Athens* is proved by the fixity of the 1755 copy by Anton Raphael Mengs at the Victoria and Albert Museum, where the rectangular framing and the consequent horizontal crop, just under the capitals of the pilasters in the foreground, exclude the entire first barrel vault and the upper portion of the sky, and thus end up suffocating the totality of the spectacle of space. Most of all, they exclude the cloudscape. As Mengs eliminates the column of air above the philosophers and crushes them against the ground, his sky becomes uniform. The space neither deepens nor expands upward. Plato's skyward gesture seems to have no space within which to move.

And so, what are Raphael's clouds doing in Bramante's *spectacle of space*? The Bramantesque spatial machinery is deliberately open to the sky and willingly constructed to react to changes in weather, recording shifts in the light. Nevertheless it remains only architecture—still, fixed, able to relate to the cloudscape only because it is integrally different. Raphael impudently fills this immobile and inanimate space, inserting the life that Bramante was too ashamed to call upon. The clouds show that the space can be used, that it can be conceived only if a time is also conceived, if we accept that it could bear a history. In fact, the passing of the clouds is the minimal trace of a history, still in its embryonic phase of a simple passing of time, of a pure unrepeatability of instants. Time passes; the clouds move; their configurations do not repeat. The same cloud could not pass twice over your head.

History, which Bramante sees substantially as a deposit of things that can be reused the moment they become useful again, like a mine of citations (as Gianfranco Contini put it regarding Dante), is for Raphael instead movement. And the possibility of understanding it is precisely the possibility of understanding how some experiences are possible *at a precise moment*. If for Bramante the collage of philosophers is an abstraction dwelling in an atemporal dimension and there is thus no need to worry about their placement in relation to a real event, for Raphael the *concordia Platonis et Aristotelis* is truly possible and therefore needs to be embodied in a real historic moment—a moment that has a specific light, in which the clouds are arranged in the sky in an unrepeatable configuration, and, precisely for this reason, is *real*. The wise men Bramante would have been happy just citing must instead meet in the reality of a calm morning. They must rest their buttocks on the marble steps of their school. History is not a warehouse of spare parts; it is a process made of moments that are still more concrete than the colossal traces they leave on the landscape. Raphael's take on Bramante is all here, in the breath of wind passing through the *spectacle of space*.

Raphael's Chigi Chapel: A Spatial Reading
Emanuel Christ

Only a painter can build like this. Everything that is physically and vividly present here in multicolored marble and plaster comes from the painterly (or perhaps rather the graphic) imagination of an artist who sees architecture primarily as a visual motif. The triumphal arch is, first and foremost, an image. The same is true of the dome's circle, the pyramid, and even the floor plan—a reproduction of Donato Bramante's cruciform floor plan for Saint Peter's Basilica. In other words, Raphael's Chigi Chapel at Santa Maria del Popolo is an architecture assembled from images and copies—a pictorial architecture that nevertheless has an astonishing, almost hallucinatory spatial effect, and in the smallest of spaces. The most important elements of this High Renaissance architectural invention are briefly addressed below.

Floor Plan: Copy and Paste

First of all, there is the floor plan. It consists of a square with chamfered corners (making it actually an octagon) with an inscribed circle. Towering in the four corners, each mighty crossing pillar is in turn divided into two columns with a niche in between, just like the monumental crossing in Saint Peter's. Here, if they are not already clear enough, the origins of this small chapel's architectural framework become obvious. Raphael simply helped himself to what he had found on his building site in the Vatican. As is well known, he was Bramante's successor there—a painter who had no architectural training whatsoever! He unceremoniously took the shape of the central structure conceived by Bramante and implanted it in the Basilica of Santa Maria del Popolo as a kind of scaled-down model (the chapel is at least ten times smaller than the crossing in Saint Peter's Basilica). This profusely bold copy-paste maneuver shows that behind this project, there was not only uninhibited imagination but also great ambition: the little chapel is competing with the largest church of them all!

This idea was not entirely new, though. To a certain extent, Bramante himself, of all people, had already provided this theme of the miniature monument only a few years earlier, in his famous Tempietto. It certainly cannot have been easy for Raphael; the smallest and largest church interiors in Rome had already been laid out by his predecessor, Bramante. Thus, it is actually clear that Raphael could only ever design in imitation of Bramante, or in an attempt to distinguish himself from him (Raphael's architecture is, after all, quite inconceivable without Bramante). Nevertheless, Raphael succeeded in inventing a completely independent new architecture. He did so by using Bramante's templates (as well as elements taken directly from images of ancient Rome, of course) and recombining them in a highly surprising way. Or would it be more accurate to say he collaged and painted them?

The Dome: Beyond Tectonics

Back to the Chigi Chapel. Rising above the equilateral floor plan and supported by four circular arches like in Saint Peter's, a round dome rests on a tambour. Its bright golden lining is in stark contrast to the chapel's otherwise rather dark materials, so via the effect of its color and light, it opens the space upward. We look up into a glittering golden firmament of paintings and architectural elements. And in the middle, the shining canopy is open. We see directly into heaven (although much of it is concealed by God). Like in the Pantheon, a circular opening in the roof extends the architectural space to infinity, albeit only as a painting in this case. This illusionistic trick probably also makes our confidence in this building's tectonic system temporarily waver a little. Moreover, the ceiling itself also acts somewhat un-architecturally: around the ceiling medallion in the middle of the dome, the coffered structure condenses to form a seemingly solid crust-like frame that appears to hang, rather than support. The roof takes on the form of a picture frame. This would have been unthinkable for Bramante.

Four Portals: The Illusion of Open Space

The termination of the three chapel walls is probably the boldest of the painterly operations because, in an architectural sense, it is actually only the portals that delimit the space. Figuratively speaking, everything in between is open. This optical depth effect is again achieved via contrasting colors and materials. The pilasters, cornices, and arches are made of light, almost white, marble. Everything between them, on the other hand—the wall linings, niches, and spandrels—is either in black and brown marble or covered with large dark paintings. This is what creates the impression of spatial depth. The painting on the central wall also contributes to this trompe l'oeil. The effect is particularly powerful if we look out of the nave through the portal (which was also copied from the Pantheon, incidentally). We can then almost imagine we are looking into the wide-open space of the *School of Athens* (1501–11) before the philosophers and scholars have arrived.

The Pyramid: Iconic Architecture

As if all this combining and contrasting were not already sufficiently thrilling, two pyramidal tombs occupy the side walls as the ultimate enhancement of the visual-spatial composition, so to speak. Here, Raphael really takes his spatial concept to the extreme, for via these two objects, the wall behind becomes a secondary matter and is, in a way, overridden. In the all-encompassing artwork of this small chapel, the pointed pyramids are the actual protagonists. They are an iconic invention of sorts, the exception in the system. With their almost aggressive presence, they positively explode the architectural framework. As in a collage, they superimpose themselves on the image in the foreground. Not only in form but also in content, they are the opposite of the lofty circular dome-and-arch architecture. According to classical tradition, the pyramid (for example the Pyramid of Cestius) refers to the realm of the dead in the underworld. Here, though, the pyramids do not even stand properly on the ground. In fact, they rest on round supports and almost seem to float! It does not take much imagination to picture them soon lifting off from their pedestals, the sarcophagi, and rising (like rockets) into the golden sky. There could hardly be a more unorthodox use of the gravest of all architectural forms. Only Barnett Newman's *Broken Obelisk* (1963–67) perhaps represents a more radical perversion of an Egyptian monument.

Metaphysical Architecture?

The pyramids are also, however, reminiscent of a painting by Giorgio de Chirico in Kunstmuseum Basel's collection, called *The Enigma of Fatality* (1914). This famous example of metaphysical painting is memorable enough for its pointed triangular shape alone. The painting's outline does indeed bear a striking resemblance to the shape of the Chigi pyramids. The connection lies not only in the painting's format, but also in its content: surrounded by arches, a room with two-colored stone slabs on the floor opens up to the sky. A red chimney (instead of the Nativity of the Virgin) occupies the center of the painting. In the foreground, a red hand reaches into the image space—perhaps like the hand of Gian Lorenzo, who intervened in Raphael's architecture with his figures while completing the Chigi Chapel in the seventeenth century because Raphael, as we know, never finished this architecture. In a sense it is still unfinished today, given the conceptual idea of openness and incompleteness it has carried within it from the very start. Raphael's architecture is more than what can be seen. In a certain way, it is metaphysical: where the architecture's physical space ends and the image's imaginary space begins.

L'ossa con la carne, or Space Is Not Enough
Victoria Easton

Raphael's art has been praised as "perfect" since Giorgio Vasari's *Lives*, where the latter uses the word at least eight times to describe Sanzio's oeuvre. Vasari sums it up in the assumption that "we have from him art, coloring, and invention harmonized and brought to such a pitch of perfection as could scarcely be hoped for; nor may any intellect ever think to surpass him," as if any vocabulary would lack enough superlatives to describe Raphael's mastery of painting.[1] The idea of perfection might be intuitively understood in regard to his painting, which most critics agree reaches a kind of apex beyond the concept of beauty.

1 "Dalle quali figure non potrebbe pittore alcuno formar cosa più leggiadra, né di maggior perfezzione"; "grandissima vivacità e colorito perfetto"; "un paese che in tutta perfezzione è singulare e bellissimo"; "con perfezzione non più da altri che da esso dipinta nella grazia del colorito"; "Il quale fece Raffaello finire con tanta perfezzione"; "la quale egli di sua mano, continuamente lavorando, ridusse ad ultima perfezzione"; "tutt'e tre le Persone unitamente ristrette nella perfezzione dell'arte di Raffaello"; "che invero noi abbiamo per lui l'arte, i colori e la invenzione unitamente ridotti a quella fine e perfezzione che appena si poteva sperare, né di passar lui già mai si pensi spirito alcuno." Giorgio Vasari, "Vita di Raffaello d'Urbino pittore et architetto," in *Le vite de' più eccellenti pittori, scultori e architettori* (Florence: Sansoni, 1906), 311–416. Translation retrieved from: Giorgio Vasari, *Lives of the Painters, Sculptors and Architects*, Trans. Gaston du C. de Vere (New York: Alfred A. Knopf, 1912), 746.

But could this mantra of perfection equally apply to Raphael's architecture? This is at least what Raphael aimed for, as he put it in a 1514 letter to his uncle—probably one of the most quoted of the few written pieces by him—where he mentions Fra Giovanni Giocondo as his mentor, "a man of the most skillful reputation, so that I may learn, if he has any beautiful secret in architecture, so that I become most perfect in this art."[2] Raphael for sure gives himself the means as he mandates a new translation of Vitruvius, which he is to personally illustrate (knowing that in the case of Raphael, *personally* means executed by some of his fifty workshop draftsmen). But he doesn't stop there, and, when designated as the surveyor of Rome's antiquities, he develops a highly accurate method to do so, which are not to be traced as such in their derelict state as ruins but in their originally intended "designs." Raphael is convinced of his aptitude to resurrect the lost according to his interpretation. But he is not satiated with a simple floor plan and section. Space was not enough; he wanted the envelope. As he complains, it only remains from Rome "the skeleton of the city as a whole, without ornaments and, so to say, *the bones of the body without flesh.*"[3]

2 Raffaello Sanzio, "Seconda lettera allo zio," 1514, in *Raffaello Sanzio. Tutti gli scritti*, (Milan: E. Camasasca, 1956). Translation retrieved from John Shearman, *Raphael in early modern sources (1483-1602)*, (New Haven / London: Yale University Press, 2003), Vol. 1, 181.

3 Raffaello Sanzio, "Lettera a Leone X," 1519, in *Raffaello Sanzio. Tutti gli scritti*, 63. English translation from Shearman, *Raphael in early modern sources (1483-1602)*, n.p.

Almost none of these surveys ever concretely happened, but his "attributed" architectural production nevertheless testifies of his eagerness to bring *everything*—or at least architecture, painting, and sculpture—together. A *Gesamtkunstwerk* before the idea was even born. Or, shall I say, "Alles ist Architektur," as Hans Hollein, one of the few possible contemporary avatars of Raphael, declared in 1967. Hollein would surely have dreamed to design the Chigi Chapel, where opulence of form, richness of material, and plethora of allegories blur the essentiality of the plan. The floor plan Uffizi 165 A is probably one of the most beautiful drawings by Raphael. Traced on graph paper, it is just a simply profiled line encircling an empty portion of the page. Reading this silhouette, one guesses his close encounter with Donato Bramante, who designed the choir in the same church, which is remarkable for its flatness, bareness, and pure use of light as the only decoration. And yet the contrast with the chapel couldn't be more striking, as Raphael tries to move past Bramante's lack of ornament and material monotony. Bramante was only bones; Raphael wanted the flesh.[4]

The origin of Raphael's sensual architecture might be traced back to his practice as a painter. A strong paradigmatic change occurred in painting in the sixteenth century, when his Madonna and her Child "descended from their pedestal to be engulfed by animated groups of familiar figures sharing their company." Then in the painting itself "the figures are not so much composed in space as joined together despite it. They look closely on one another, stare myopically into eyes and at flesh, grasp, embrace, hold and finger each other's bodies as if their recognition rested more firmly on touch than on sight."[5] In which terms does this descent of the Madonna into a plebeian world—far away from any social distancing—and which Raphael intentionally propagated, reflect into his architecture?

4 "Ché, avegna che a' dì nostri l'architectura sia molto svegliata e venuta assai proxima alla maniera delli antichi, come si vede per molte belle opere di Bramante, niente di meno li ornamenti non sono di materia tanto preziosa come li antichi, che con infinita spesa par che mettessero ad effetto ciò che imaginarno e che solo el volere rompesse ogni difficultate." Raffaello Sanzio, "Lettera a Leone X," 63.

5 Robin Evans, "Figures, Doors and Passages," in *Translations from Drawing to Building and Other Essays* (1978; repr., London: MIT Press, 1997), 58–59.

Let's take Raphael's words at face value, and assume that architecture's flesh is ornament, which is one of his main architectural tools. Since Leon Battista Alberti theorized it, ornament is considered an entity dissociated from structure, but on the other hand, it isn't merely filling. Ornament was the tool with which Raphael became a painter of structure and with which he dared to elude conventions with an excuse: *this is only ornament*. In the Psyche Loggia, the greenery becomes fake trusses, an interweave of plants festoons—a kind of greenwashing avant la lettre—where light, color, perspective, and trompe l'oeil altogether achieve an immersive experience, letting the ceiling dissolve into space. The pictorial decoration is stronger than Baldassarre Peruzzi's architecture, not only as a pattern, but because it manages to link to the external space of the garden and become part of a bigger whole. In the Chigi Chapel, the side walls are embellished with a checkerboard made of two different marbles, which the two unadorned and abstract pyramids brutally cover, even breaking the borders of the frame. But instead of using a different marble for the pyramids, Raphael used the same as the one of the grid, blurring the spatiality of the geometrical intruder. The flattening effect of the material contrasts with the protruding effect of the pyramid and shows masterfulness as well as ambiguity. The chapel is a completely autonomous object within the church, but one is tempted to touch its all-encompassing *fleshness* like one would caress the descended Madonna.

This desecration of space results in a very inclusive architecture, one of unexpected generosity that might feel "perfectly complete." *Perfectio* literally means "a finishing." Raphael's spaces are indeed finished. Nothing needs to be added, no questions are left to be answered, everybody agrees. But in front of this indescribable and unequaled evidence, one might be left to consider Raphael's architectural work, as Henri Focillon puts it, "both heavenly and insignificant."[6]

6 "à la fois céleste et insignifiant," Henri Focillon, *Raphaël* (Paris: Editions Nilsson, 1926), 12.

Light from Above
Bruce Boucher

There's a pen and red chalk drawing by Raphael of the cornice inside the Pantheon. It is a simple, quick sketch that captures the essence of the moldings as they catch the light from above, and it must be one of a number of similar sketches of that iconic building, which no longer survive. The red chalk gives a glow to the profile that caught the artist's eye, and even at a distance of five hundred years, it seems to radiate off the page. Like all Renaissance artists, Raphael was sensitive to the fall of light, both in his paintings but also on the facades and interiors of chapels, villas, and palaces. Consider, for example, the *bugnato gentile* of the facade of Palazzo Alberini, which recalls Bramante's Palazzo Caprini, also known as the House of Raphael, where the artist lived during his later years in Rome. Sunlight brings out the horizontal and vertical patterns that animate the astylar facade in the absence of a canonical order. Its kinship with Palazzo Caprini can be seen in the modernized treatment of the shops and mezzanines above them while the *piano nobile* is elegant in its understatement, with *lesene* instead of an engaged order.

The one disservice that Giorgio Vasari did to Raphael was to marginalize his work as an architect in his relatively detailed account of the artist's life in the *Vite.*[1] It was the work of scholars in the second half of the twentieth century to recover a sense of the sweep and engagement Raphael felt in this field, and if he and Pope Leo X de Medici had lived longer, then the Villa Madama and new Saint Peter's would have been manifestos of a richer, *all'antica* style, with more attention to color and decorative details—elements that Raphael found lacking in the example of Bramante.

1 Giorgio Vasari, *Le vite de' più eccellenti pittori, scultori e architettori* (Florence: 1568).

Of course, the Pantheon exerted a great fascination over artists and antiquarians alike, but for Raphael the appeal resulted in an intensive period of study and absorption of its many details that distinguished it among ancient Roman buildings then standing. This can be seen in the Chigi Chapel at Santa Maria del Popolo, a miniature homage to the Pantheon in which the central plan surmounted by a dome is enriched by colored marbles, bronze reliefs, statues, and mosaics. Raphael was close to the patron, the wealthy Agostino Chigi, who supported this essay in re-creating the richness of classical architecture, and the artist pulled out all the stops. Here, light pours in from the lantern above, creating a symbolic source of salvation. Although left incomplete by Raphael, the chapel was rightly understood by Gian Lorenzo Bernini a century later as an early example of the *Gesamtkunstwerk*, or total work of art, in which all elements were subordinated to the vision of the creator. Bernini's interpolations not only completed the work, but also built upon the example of Raphael, where light and color are modulated and become a metaphor of ascension of the spirit.

Raphael experimented with similar ideas in another Chigi project, the Farnesina, a villa created by Baldassarre Peruzzi in Trastevere near the banks of the Tiber. His interventions were confined to frescoes, such as the celebrated Galatea and the tour de force of the Psyche Loggia. There the frescoes relate the legend of Cupid and Psyche as told by the late Roman writer Apuleius, in which Psyche finally triumphs over her persecution by Venus. Raphael conceived the loggia as an open-air pergola in which the aerial actions of the gods take place above our heads, with Mercury appearing to fly from one side of the space to another. Originally, the room was unglazed so that it had the appearance of a liminal space between the garden and the rest of the villa, possibly conjuring up a *macchina da festa* to celebrate the wedding of Chigi and his bride, Francesca Ordeaschi.

Raphael's great talent as a painter and architect was given great scope in papal Rome, but one of his most important commissions is also probably the least well known. This was the series of tapestries woven in Flanders but destined to cover the walls of the Sistine Chapel. The commission came from Leo X, and both the patron and the destination marked them out for serious attention. The pope pitted the talent of Raphael against that of his older rival within the Sistine Chapel. The tapestries were intended to be hung over the lower sections of the walls, beneath the late fifteenth-century frescoes of the lives of Moses and Jesus and directly below the recently completed masterpiece of Michelangelo's ceiling. Their subject matter comes from the Acts of the Apostles and completes the narrative that begins on the ceiling with the creation of the world and Adam and Eve, followed by the stories of Moses and Christ, concluding with the spreading of the gospel by Peter and Paul. Raphael's tapestries were aligned with the narrative frescoes on the walls above and are embellished by decorative panels. To achieve the desired effect, Raphael altered his style toward larger figures and broader gestures, more like a modern billboard. Although somewhat dulled by time, the gold and silver threads of the tapestries still glimmer as they did when they were briefly rehung in the Sistine Chapel last February to mark the five hundredth anniversary of Raphael's death (2020).

Grotesque
Manuel Orazi

Pictoribus atque poetis quidlibet audendi semper fuit aequa potestas.
—Horace, *Ars poetica*[1]

1 "poets and painters [you will say] have ever had equal authority for attempting any thing." http://www.perseus.tufts.edu/hopper/text?doc=Perseus%3Atext%3A1999.02.0065

No artist has been as nullifying as Raphael. In fact, late Romantic culture used the term Pre-Raphaelite not only and not so much as an adjective, but as an authentic category of the spirit. Even Alois Riegl, so immune to singular personalities, chose him as the historiographical divide for his *Historical Grammar of the Visual Arts* (2008). The work of the artist from Urbino not only had a posthumous effect; to measure his impact on his contemporaries, it is enough to compare two works by Lorenzo Lotto, both produced at Recanati. The distance between the first, *The Recanati Polyptych* (1508), and the second, *The Transfiguration* (1512), is immeasurable; they appear to be by the hands of two different artists. The stylistic trepidation of the first, perhaps due to his crypto-Protestantism, is completely absent in the second, painted after his Roman sojourn in 1509, when he worked in close contact with Raphael and the other artists of the court of Pope Julius II. Lotto's exacerbated frescoes were not appreciated by the "warrior pope," who was then searching for an imperial-style Classicism—an *instauratio urbis* and at the same time *restitutio antiquitatis.* Hence, they were erased and substituted by those, precisely, of Raphael. The disorientation of the Venetian painter, as errant as he was heretic, was thus definitive; he would never again return to Rome. And returning home, around the Marches, he stopped in Umbria to see the works of Sanzio and his master, Pietro Perugino, bending to their manner for the *Transfiguration* of Recanati, albeit with some reluctance.

Raphael's architectural work is instead concentrated in his last nine years (1511–20), and even if its multiplicity makes it difficult to identify a single style, we can say that he was aiming not only to "rediscover the beautiful forms of antiquity" but, most of all, at "the coincidence between Beauty and Truth within the rational harmony of the Rule" in the alveus of a general synthesis of the arts.[2] The composure of his architectonic oeuvre, prefigured in the painted architectures that are the background of his first works, such as the temple with the centralized plan in the *Marriage of the Virgin* (1504) or the invention of the Venetian window in *The Fire in the Borgo* (1514), is discursive and not assertive as in the case of Donato Bramante, who perhaps was his uncle. "Apodictic, even in his experimentalism, is Bramante's language; colloquial is Raphael's."[3] The Raphaelesque course of action is therefore a constant elaboration of details of the Roman in terms of an author's variation, which did not exclude quotes of more recent experiences, such as the cone-covered dome of the Chigi Chapel in Santa Maria del Popolo, inspired by the dome of Urbino's San Bernardino by Francesco di Giorgio.

2 Stefano Ray, "Il volo di Icaro. Raffaello, architettura e cultura," in *Raffaello architetto*, ed. Christoph Luitpold Frommel, Stefano Ray, and Manfredo Tafuri (Milan: Electa 1984), 57.

3 Manfredo Tafuri, "'Roma instaurata'. Strategie urbane e politiche pontificie nella Roma del primo Cinquecento," in *Raffaello architetto*, 63.

"Nothing is more 'Raphael' than that dome," writes Cesare Brandi.[4] Colloquial, that is to say profane and modern, was his way of managing intellectual, artistic, and professional relations. By no means arduous were his exchanges with scholars such as Baldassarre Castiglione, even less with his collaborators, particularly painter-architects like him, for instance Giulio Romano and Baldassarre Peruzzi, who would never completely bend to the manner of the master, preserving their own inclinations. Others would specialize, like Giovanni da Udine, a virtuoso in drawing animals and especially grotesques, a taste that spread like wildfire through Europe thanks to the work of Flemish engravers—in Flanders even tapestries were reproducing the Raphaelesque cartoons. According to the young Manfredo Tafuri, the work of Raphael and of his circle on the synthesis of the arts has mainly been formulated thanks to the discovery of the ancient "grotesques," a type of work suitable for fast-paced group execution. Still, the Olympian calm of Sanzio and, in a final analysis, his highly decanted Classicism were therefore mined at the most superficial level, that is, the decorative, as can be seen in the Farnesina and the Vatican loggias as well as in Villa Madama.

4 Cesare Brandi, *Disegno dell'architettura italiana* (Rome: Castelvecchi, 2013), 196.

Not by chance, Vitruvius condemned this oneiric kind of ornamentation that caused, according to André Chastel, the negation of space and the fusion of species, the lack of gravity of form and the insolent proliferation of *hybrids*. From here, hence, emerges the classic contrast between the courtly grace, "voluptuous and light," of Raphael and the solitary and nicodemite tragic nature of Michelangelo, his antagonist both in the synthesis of the arts and in nonchalance. Well known is the passage by Venetian scholar Lodovico Dolce, writing in 1557:

I know that at Rome, while Raphael was living, the learned, and the most skilful artists there, preferred him to Michelangelo as a painter, and that those who held him inferior, were for the most part sculptors, who considered only Michelangelo's excellence in design, and the forcible air of his figures, esteeming the graceful and gentle manner of Raphael too easy, and consequently not so artificial, not knowing that ease is the highest accomplishment of any art, and the most difficult to be attained, that hiding art is the utmost extent of art, and that other elements are absolutely necessary to constitute a painter besides design.[5]

5 Lodovico Dolce, *Aretin: A Dialogue on Painting from the Italian of Lodovico Dolce* (London: Printed for P. Elmsley, 1770), 13–14.

According to Nikolaus Pevsner, Classicism corresponds not to a precise style, as do Gothic or Romanesque, but to an aesthetic behavior; or perhaps we are dealing with another category of spirit, that precisely of some architects born in the 1970s (Dogma, Office Kersten Geers David Van Severen, 51N4E, LAN, Christ & Gantenbein, Baukuh et al.). Then again, enantiodromia is also a quality among great artistic personalities. Hence, to the Renaissance Classicism of Raphael can be opposed the group work of the grotesques—figures, precisely anti-Renaissance, characterized by a "mixture of rigor and inconsistency that made one think of a dream."[6] It is no surprise that Daniele Barbaro, mentor and patron of that other champion of Classicism, Palladio, in his *Vitruvian Commentaries* of 1556 had already reduced them, and not without reason, to *picturae somnium*, a dream of painting as deprecated by Renaissance classicists as impregnated with an infinite and tenuous allure.

6 André Chastel, *La Gotesque* (Paris: La Promeneur, 1988), n.p.

Roman Architecture
Kersten Geers

According to Giorgio Vasari, Raphael was born in Urbino "at three o'clock of the night on Good Friday" in 1483, and died exactly thirty-seven years later "on the same day that he was born, which was Good Friday." A coincidence worthy of his divine talent, his death seemed part of an elaborate plan. Sudden high fever, rumored to be the result of his excessive lifestyle and subsequent incorrectly used bloodletting, contributed to his untimely death. Still, he had enough time (and power and connections) to arrange to be buried in the Pantheon, the Roman monument rechristened as Santa Maria Rotonda. In some way it perfectly matched the license Raphael seemed to have acquired in his short life as artist and architect around anything Roman, and by extension everything Raphaelesque.

At the time of Raphael's death in 1520, it had been only six years since Donato Bramante had died. The gigantic construction site in the Vatican, initiated by Bramante with the eradication of the old Saint Peter's basilica, had been some fifteen years under way. The *cantiere* of Saint Peter's and the Belvedere was a ruin at best, albeit one subject to an inverse dynamic. Bramante's grandiose "Roman" project, an attempt to rebuild the Vatican according to the principles of the ancients, was somehow successful purely by means of the mess it made. As an instant ruin, vaguely reminiscent of the Circo Massimo, it was Roman by default. The death of its initiator gave it an air of historical inevitability, only furthered by the Belvedere's infrastructural outset and the four executed colossal piers of Saint Peter's basilica. The successive "versions" by Raphael, Baldassarre Peruzzi, Antonio da Sangallo the Younger, and later Michelangelo endlessly oscillated between construction, reconstruction, interpretation, and transformation, and thus somehow automatically guaranteed any outcome a Roman pedigree. Bramante's *all'antico* was a conceptual affair, with building *ex nihilo* at its core. Emulating Rome's imperial and territorial tendencies, it developed an abstract and simple architecture as the intelligent consequence of a forced circumstance: Roman architecture here stood for pragmatism after tabula rasa.

Twelve years earlier, in 1508, Raphael had come to Rome, invited by Pope Julius II and probably on the recommendation of Bramante, to paint a cycle of frescoes in the Vatican apartments overlooking the Belvedere construction site. Upon his arrival, Raphael made a set of drawings of the Pantheon, also then one of the most remarkable ancient Roman monuments. It is a drawing with curious detail. Part spatial evocation, part syntactic document, it shows the Pantheon in a simplified and confident manner with utmost spatial and evocative effect. By changing the orders and shortening the sequence of tabernacles and exedra, it distills forms, tropes, and particularities in an accumulation of architectural features that are carefully edited to show the architectural *idea* of the Pantheon. John Shearman wrote (in 1968), after listing the slight but significant differences between the real and the idealized Pantheon, the drawing and the building: "The only explanation that I can offer is that he felt [it] looked better that way."[1]

1 John Shearman, *Journal of the Royal Society of Arts*, April 1968, Vol. 116, No. 5141: 401.

From the moment Raphael arrived in Rome, he started developing his own stance toward the ancient architecture of the eternal city based on an erudite but edited (and thus selective) accumulation of ancient tropes. He was a collector of knowledge. His proficiency culminated when he was appointed Rome's commissioner of antiquities and wrote the now-famous letter to Pope Leo X soliciting protection of the ancient architecture, of what was left after the barbarism of earlier generations who shamelessly redeployed anything they might find as material for new construction. In order to preserve, one should idealize, and in order to idealize, one should accumulate, with rigor and a good measure of science, but also (and here I paraphrase Shearman) with license. Even if Raphael ultimately developed his own architecture from the shared architectural obsessions of Bramante's *bottega*, it seems it was his specific embrace of formal license—the possibility to interpret and tweak an inherent syntax in everything ancient he studied—by which he made Roman architecture his own. The drawing of the Pantheon is not a wrong or a simplified rendition of the Pantheon; it is simply *his* Pantheon.

In the years Raphael worked under Pope Leo X, his architecture embraced a bigger scale. In many ways, Villa Madama, whose construction started in 1519, is his own Belvedere, in both scale and ambition. Built on the outskirts of Rome, it was to be an accumulation of any possible Roman trope in one gigantic building complex, a contemporary Hadrian's Villa. Ironically, and perhaps as the immediate consequence of such a grand ambition, construction stopped with Raphael's death, and became a fata morgana of impossible-to-attain Romanness. The Belvedere and Saint Peter's basilica, Bramante's own impossible Roman ruins, were both finished over time, something their brutal presence and open authorship seemingly made inevitable.

In hindsight, Raphael's more sophisticated architecture of accumulation and appropriation was also more vulnerable, as it was intrinsically connected to his (and Giulio Romano's) own license, and deeply intertwined with the *maniera* of its author. When the author died, the building vanished. The inverted tactic of imposed authorship, inherent to the act of editing, collecting, and accumulating, requires smart timing and immediate action. It was an insight Raphael honored on his deathbed when he paid for one of the ancient tabernacles in the Rotonda to be restored so he could be buried in it. Curating sometimes only requires a name. The Pantheon is Raphael's most important building.

A Letter to the Youth
Antonio Cataldo

Raphael. The Vatican's museums. One of my first teenage study trips to the Italian capital, accompanied by a lot of hormonal emotions and most probably inebriation—typical mischief for such long school journeys. Today I think that these youthful memories are probably less individual than I once imagined, as I came to see how a generation shares the same recollections. An intertwined subjectivity is formed through public school learning and socially determined habits, including such little escapades beyond the strict nets thrown upon us by society. We, who studied art as our main subject in high school, all embraced the unquestioned aesthetic authority of the art historian Giulio Carlo Argan, whose name we glorified because the academic circles of students years ahead of us also glorified it, and they had made a step in life most of us would never manage due to the societal conditions underpinning both our origins and our apparent consequent ambitions. We were, after all, small-town students from mostly precarious, low-income, working families—the kind idealized by upper-class intellectuals such as Pier Paolo Pasolini for belonging to vanishing livelihoods. Inadvertently, we were instead trapped in a condition repeating itself like an infinite-mirror effect.

It is for these basic, obvious reasons that we certainly didn't share the same conditions or networks as Argan, nor origins in Turin, the first Italian capital under King Victor Emmanuel II, who brought to the South, as Antonio Gramsci analyzed, different forms of colonization and expropriation. Argan joined the ranks of the Fascist party in 1928 (contrary to Gramsci, who was imprisoned by the regime and didn't survive it), and as a wunderkind he obtained a number of prestigious assignments. After the war, he transitioned, like so many intellectuals, to the PCI (Italian Communist Party), and was acquitted of his political sins by its leader, Palmiro Togliatti, without having to submit to even the slightest penance.

Argan then wrote *Storia dell'Arte Italiana* (1968), our "art history bible," and that's why I know of him. It must have been in its pages that I first saw, learned about, and admired the work of Raphael. Raphael, he who "is the one who most clearly placed art as an end in itself or, at least, as an activity that cannot draw on its ultimate ends unless it is first realized and justified as art."[1] The same book emphasizes that Raphael's years in Rome are central to the definition of Classicism as "a serene possession of a unitary conception of world."[2] The ambition to capture the all-encompassing known world within one ideology, despite the number of lives it cost to build it, to canonize it, to evangelize it, is a perverse credo. This is probably the reason why we were taught, as the people's students, to start distinguishing between the "man" and the "intellectual," the artwork and the life of the artist. Now I realize, these many years later, how important this separation was for so much to be justified. It was in this split between the persona and the representation that certain dogmas could be perpetrated and endless questions around the life of (in)famous men could be dismissed.

1 Giulio Carlo Argan, *Storia dell'Arte Italiana* (Florence: Sansoni, 1968), 428. Unless otherwise noted, all translations are rendered by the author.
2 Ibid, 427.

Today I would ask: Was Raphael not aware of the Church's violent evangelizing role and how far it reached? Was he not aware of the Church's blessing to Christopher Columbus? Was he not aware of the genocide of fifty-five to one hundred million people that Columbus's conquering of the Americas would bring about? Was he not aware of these realities when he painted Columbus in 1509, a portrait to be hung alongside those of other "illustrious" men in the Vatican? Was he not aware that his images were helping to build a new worldview—a world whose borders were enlarging under his eye but whose view was to be canonized under one single ideal, that of the Church?

Julius II, nicknamed the "warrior pope" and known as the "greatest art patron of the papal line," launched a far-reaching building program that was at the same time an economic, political, and ideological restructuring.[3] *Renovatio* was a model for a more "perfect" urban life (*civitas*) in the face of the reality of conflict, rivalry, and religious and political crises. Giles of Viterbo, spokesperson for Julius II, delivered a lengthy oration on December 21, 1507, the Feast of Saint Thomas, at Saint Peter's Basilica. Julius II had received celebratory news from King Manuel I of Portugal concerning his trading interests in the Far East, spanning Ceylon (Sri Lanka), Calicut (Kozhikode), and Madagascar. These celebrations happened not by chance on that particular day: Saint Thomas himself allegedly evangelized Syrian Christians in India, and this interlacing with biblical storytelling allowed Julius II to demonstrate an uninterrupted Christian empire of faith, leading to a whole new world order, guided by his vision.[4] The *renovatio urbis*, a moral edification of the highest terms of trade, beauty, and lawfulness, underpinned the artistic and humanistic culture of Julius II. Raphael seems to have been both instrumental to these ideals and to have deferred to them. His art contains a unity of the contingent and the transcendent that can be immediately understood, and that became and remained popular, according to Argan. It was the official art of the Church at a time when "to defend the evidence of revelation against the anxiety of the religious problem" was of fundamental importance.[5]

3 Massimo Rospocher, *Il papa guerriero. Giulio II nello spazio pubblico europeo* (Bologna: Il Mulino, 2015), 71. Pope Julius II was elected in 1503. His urban restructuring took as its premise the urban programs of Nicholas V and Sixtus IV. Rome regained its status as the administrative and financial driving force of what was happening in the various provinces subjected directly or indirectly to pontifical authority, assuming its own physiognomy, also in terms of urban development, as the capital city. On the situation of the city of Rome in the context of the overall structure of the ecclesiastical state, its symbolic values, and the transformations that affected its urban development see *Via Giulia. Un'utopia urbanistica del '500*, ed. Luigi Salerno, Luigi Spezzaferro, and Manfredo Tafuri (Rome: Staderini, 1973); Manfredo Tafuri, "'Roma instaurata.' Strategie urbane e politiche pontificie nella Roma del primo '500," in *Raffaello Architetto*, ed. Christoph L. Frommel, Stefano Ray, and Manfredo Tafuri (Milan: Electa, 1984), 59–106.

4 "It remains for us to recognize what King Manuel of Portugal has given these people [of India and Ceylon] in bringing them the branches of [Julius II's] tree. [. . .] Manuel, conquer of Ceylon and the Bay of Bengal, is wreathed with oak leaves, for together with the golden oak he brings them a golden age." Francis X. Martin, *Friar, Reformer, and Renaissance Scholar: Life and Work of Giles of Viterbo, 1469–1532* (Villanova, PA: Augustinian, 1992), cited in Nicholas Temple, "Renovatio Urbis: Giles of Viterbo and the 'Golden Age' of Julius II," paper presented at the 14th International European Association of Urban History Conference: "Urban Renewal and Resilience: Cities in Comparative Perspective," Rome, August 31, 2018, https://www.academia.edu/37077006/Renovatio_Urbis_Giles_of_Viterbo_and_the_Golden_Age_of_Julius_II

5 "Compito dell'artista non è di correggere la sembianza illusoria, ma di dimostrare la verità delle sembianze. È proprio per questa unità di contingente e trascendente nella solare evidenza della forma che l'arte di Raffaello è stata capita, è diventata subito ed è rimasta popolare; ed è stata l'arte ufficiale della Chiesa." Argan, *Storia dell'arte Italiana*, 447.

When Raphael, at the height of his fame, portrayed Julius II—in what is considered a significant turning point in such depictions through inserting the psychological aspect of the subject—didn't he know he would humanize, and hence justify, such a figure, almost as a victim of his humanity? How should we read the image(s) he produced for us?

Art critic Carla Lonzi, who attacks Argan's "heterodirectional" and hyper-privileged approach, attempts to deconstruct such ideologically driven positions coming not only from the artist but also equally by the chief mediator of the artwork.[6] The critic, according to Lonzi, has to share with the historical personality who lived the experience the risk of the artists, "the same internal reasons."[7]

She expresses dissent toward academic criticism and its undue contiguity between "life" and "ideology."[8] For Lonzi, academic art criticism is unreliable in many ways. Critical activity can only survive to bear witness through argumentative levels that intertwine intimate memoir and historical investigation.[9] I would phrase it as questioning and moving between a given collective subjectivity, a subjective identity, and subjectivity itself.

6 Carla Lonzi, "Jean Fautrier, la pittura informale e la 'chose vue,'" *L'approdo letterario* 5 (January–March 1959): 136–38. For this and for other cited contributions of Carla Lonzi see also Michele Dantini, "Una polemica situata e da situare. Dicembre 1963: Lonzi vs Argan," in *Arte italiana 1960–1964. Identità culturale, confronti internazionali, modelli americani*, ed. Flavio Fergonzi, Francesco Tedeschi (Milan: Scalpendi, 2017), 105–20.

7 Carla Lonzi, "Michel Tapié e la mostra 'Strutture e stile' al Museo d'Arte Moderna di Torino," *L'approdo letterario* 8, no. 19 (July–September 1962): 159.

8 Carla Lonzi, "Mostra della critica italiana 1961," *L'approdo letterario* 8, nos. 17/18 (January–June 1962): 214–15.

9 Carla Lonzi, "Solitudine di un critico," *Avanti!*, December 13, 1963: 23.

Image reproduction technologies helped foster even further a quotidian affection for and capillary distribution of power and ideology; photography was instrumental in building mythologies. It is in this repetition, in the construction of a mass culture without a critical perspective, that Raphael becomes important more for what he represents as a figure and a constructed hero and less for the content of his work. It is here, in witnessing the indulgence of his work as such, that we find the quintessential lesson to overturn the paradigm Argan tried to establish about art per se. Art per se, as a dogma of the Catholic Church, becomes true in its empty repetition, with no explanation needed. The power of the dogma lies in leaving it unquestioned every single day, literally by not finding another angle, another still-unknown point of the story. It is the literalness of photography against the literalness of the repetition, the witness against the document, the quotidian against history, today against yesterday.

In the Mind's Eye
Maddalena Scimemi

Eight handwritten pages from the State Archive in Florence, bearing neither author nor header, translate into words the plan of the great residence at the doors of Rome willed for by Pope Leo X. A villa *all'antica*, intended for the cardinal Giulio de' Medici and located on the slopes of Mount Mario: its construction, begun in the summer of 1518, would occupy Raphael over the course of his last, intense year of life. Not until the spring of 1522 would it be used for the first time, and that would occur without Raphael and without the pontiff, who had passed away a few months earlier.

The date of the document oscillates between the winter of 1518 and that of 1519, and shared opinion believes it a copy of an original by Raphael, which passed through the hands of Baldassarre Castiglione for the scholar from Mantua to affix his additions. The villa's ekphrasis, inspired by the descriptions of villas in Pliny the Younger's *Epistulae*, is the fruit of sophisticated and contemplated choices. The writer adopts Latin terms and translates them into Italian, and he follows a precise hierarchy in describing the different spaces, both open and closed, always advancing the reasons determining their position and form, clarifying their geometry and dimensions of each space. The reader is engrossed by the account, which has a strong cinematic component: line after line, we feel as if we are visiting the villa arm in arm with the writer, being led from a courtyard to an inner room, then back out into the garden, only to enter again, changing rooms and following the light, pushing ourselves all the way to the parapet of the loggia to look out onto the void and contemplate the river, the fields, and Rome. Were it not anachronistic, one could imagine that his words aimed to simulate an *ante litteram* filmic experience. We are dealing with a documentary source with a nonlinear interpretation—a priceless source that acts like a web of golden threads in which different characters are caught, events connected, meanings interwoven. Since in reality only a fragment of Villa Madama exists—it has been left incomplete since 1527—and so the document constitutes an essential source for understanding the project in its entirety.

At the moment of its writing, if we accept the earlier date, the architecture was not yet discernible, but something could be intuited. In fact, at the end of 1518, the terracing of the available grounds, gently waning to the banks of the Tevere, was already being levelled. Works began at the point where a large fish pond was planned, coordinating the earthworks with the excavations of the basin and the canalizations, erecting substructures and foundation walls. This was a strategic construction site, providing the pope, first and foremost, with a panoramic terrace where he could banquet with his guests in the open air, entertained by ornamental water features, sculptures of ancient divinities, and exotic animals.

The terrace with the fish pond, facing the *oriente equinoziale*, would take advantage of the topography of Mount Mario to revel in the favorable winds and the sun's rays. At a lower level with respect to the apartments, accessible by an open staircase and connected to a secret kitchen, it would rest against a deep and narrow substructure wall, dug from three recesses, interconnected and walkable thanks to an open passage in the thickness of the buttresses. Sebastiano Serlio would praise the effectiveness of the structural solution in his Book IV, and in the Royal Institute of British Architects collection there is a precious drawing by Andrea Palladio dedicated to Villa Madama in which the terracing is rendered in plan and in elevation.

Let us return to the letter, where the terrace is described in a relatively quick passage compared with those of other parts, of which details abound: *Et infine della scala volta a Maestro ha a lato l'acqua una cenatione, molto delectevole et per il fresco e per la veduta* (And at the end of the stairway facing the Mistral and beside the water, there is a *cenatione*, delectable for its coolness and for its view). Few words suffice for what probably, already in 1518, was the most readable point of the entire construction site. The text reports a *cenatione*, an open-air dining area, at a lower height—as, in effect, it is—but places it at the northern extremity of the fish pond, or rather, farther away from the villa than it really is.

The speed of this passage and the new, more convenient placement from a functional point of view are therefore the clues that tell of a defined yet flexible system, in which adjustments are determined by considerations also of a practical order, able to maintain the logic of the system itself—a panoramic room, set apart, cool, with a pool and ornamental water features—by reconfiguring its form.

At the same time, the eccentric position of the *cenatione*, described in the letter and later abandoned, identifies a precise moment in the genesis of the project. In a flash we can glimpse the intersection of Raphael's deep understanding of antiquity and the creativity of his inventions. Well known in the correspondence of Pietro Bembo is the passage in which the Venetian humanist announced, in the spring of 1516, a gentlemen's trip to the antiquities of Tivoli in the company of Raphael. Thirty years would pass before Pirro Ligorio, Neapolitan architect and archaeologist, identified Hadrian as the commissioner of the complex, recognizing in the ruins, at the far end of a long valley, the temple of Canopo, adorned with marble statues and water features. But this does not exclude that in the second decade of the sixteenth century, when archaeological knowledge of the villa was still dawning, that those ruins could stimulate Raphael to "invent" the open-air *triclinium* and situate it in its first position, at the opposite end of the terracing with respect to the villa.

If in the case of the *cenatione* we can compare the text with the realized solution, another reading of the letter proves crucial for understanding the importance of what, in reality, would never be built, and what, if we limit ourselves to how much appears in the two drawings conserved in the Uffizi, may appear to be a marginal detail.[1] In the calibrated sequence that underpins the description in the letter, the first architectural structure chosen to introduce the entire complex is that of a great round tower, gracing the entrance with *belezza et superbia*, erected in the most exposed point of the site, halfway from the mountain. Reading these lines, it seems as if the breath of the *grecho* is upon us, that cold and dry wind that on certain clear days comes from the northeast.

1 The Uffizi drawings are GDSU 273 A *recto* and GDSU 314 A *recto*.

Above the great tower, six *canne* in diameter, the letter describes a completely windowed round space. It is set apart, located at the extreme corner of a garden that smells of *melangholi* (oranges) and is invigorated by the gurgling of a fountain that takes its waters from the *vena viva*. The garden itself is isolated from the sumptuous sequence of courtyards and apartments of the villa, despite being located right behind the main entrance: upstream, a high wall impedes the view of whoever is crossing the *lochi pubblici*; downstream, it is protected by a narrow and long *andito,* a covered passage that finishes precisely at the cornered central tower.

Even if the great tower serves *anchora a un poco de difesa* (still as a bit of defense), in reality it is a small pavilion, a space "in which it is very pleasant to stay." The low rays of the winter sun, with the passing of the hours, touch the *invetriate* openings one after the other, turning, *intorno intorno . . . traspaiono*, granting a view of Rome at midday, and to the east the gentle meanders of the Tevere. The pavilion is defined as *dyeta . . . alegrissima* for its light and for its view. There are ancient precedents of towered villas: for instance the residences facing Mount Argentario and overlooking the Tyrrhenian coast of the Ager Cosanus, a territory well known to Raphael and his collaborators. But none of the small towers of these ancient villas can host a living space within. Instead, the letter describes hanging gardens with a parapet facing the landscape and a narrow passage with a hybrid corner tower/*dyeta* at an extremity, evoking and distilling the experience of the palaces of Urbino, Pienza, of the villas of Fiesole, and even of a Roman precedent, that of the small room located in the corner at the *viridarium* of Palazzo Venezia.

It is in this space, of the proportions of a small casino (the diameter is just slightly greater than six meters), where gentlemen would gather to reason during the coldest season, the letter announced strategically. Translating this into modern lexicon, we could define it as a small *belvedere*, a gate lodge, a sort of *fumoir ante litteram*. Imagining the guests, even today, is not difficult: they are the protagonists of an elite immortalized in Raphael's portraits: first among them the pope and his ambassador, Giulio de' Medici, followed by Castiglione himself, the secretary Bembo, the datary Baldassarre Turini, and the cardinals closest to the Medici court. It seems incredible that, given the choice between the circular court, a Vitruvian atrium, the open-air theater, the summer loggia, the small thermal baths, and, obviously, the *cenatione*, the conversing of the gentlemen is referred to this small and isolated room, even with its spectacular view. Yet still, this choice represents the perfect portrait of Raphael the architect.

Even without the construction—as in the case of the *dyeta dello inverno*, which is intelligible thanks to its description in the letter—the spark of Raphael's invention continues to shine beyond the document.

Raphael's Spatial Fantasies in the Garden of Villa Madama
Frank Boehm

Fragment and Fantasy

Although Villa Madama—as it presents itself today—remains impressive, it is only part of a larger project that was never completed. For centuries, this unfulfilled intention has captured the imagination. Its singular fascination derives from its total lack of constitutive elements. As the structure was only half completed, we experience a semicircular, unintended forecourt instead of the planned circular inner courtyard. The outdoor facilities, planned as additions, are largely missing. Nevertheless, it is said that Villa Madama is one of the very few modern buildings in Rome of which Andrea Palladio made a scale drawing. What spatial effect would a fully realized building have had in the context of these extensive grounds?

Drawing as Manifesto

Raphael's contribution to architecture is well known, yet it is largely overshadowed by his reputation as a painter and draftsman.[1] His architectural designs have either not been realized, realized only in fragments, reworked, or destroyed by others. Drawings for his architectural projects are also rare and usually from other sources. There is simply a lack of references. An exception is the drawing *Progetto delle terrazze dei giardini per Villa Madama* from around 1518, which resides in the Gabinetto disegni e stampe in the Gallerie degli Uffizi.[2] The only drawing clearly attributed to him does not concern the villa itself, but a section of the exterior. Against the background of Raphael's devotion to antiquity, as expressed in his letter to Leone X of 1519, this drawing constitutes a completely independent radicalism.[3]

1 Angelamaria Aceto, Francesco P. di Teodoro, "L'architettura disegnata. Nuove indagini e prospettive per 'Raffaello architetto,'" in *Raffaello 1520–1483*, ed. Marzia Faietti, Matteo Lafranconi (Milan: Skira, 2020), 317–29.

2 The Uffizi inventory number is inv. 1356 Ar.

3 Raffaello Sanzio, "Lettera a Leone X," 1519, in *Raffaello Sanzio. Tutti gli scritti*, ed. Ettore Camesasca (Milan: Rizzoli, 1956), n.p.

Pure Geometry

The drawing presents the ground plan of a series of three spaces, largely without context. A square at the top is followed by a circle in the middle and an ellipse below, with the two focal points spaced apart to match the exact diameter of the segments of the circle. In contrast to the courtyards inscribed in the building's volumes, these spaces, limited only by walls, push against each other in the drawing. The outlines of the basic geometric forms touch each other directly, and the three-part composition is radically reduced. When we consider that this complex was probably not intended to be realized in direct spatial connection to the villa—research does not unanimously agree on the precise location—but was to be projected onto the surrounding landscape, the consistent formal language becomes obvious.[4] The pure square placed on nature—a concept of appropriation of urban origin—is then transformed through spatial development into a circle, which in turn mutates into an ellipse, a square extended by two semicircles. A visitor enjoying the villa's park would be partaking in a geometry lesson.

4 The connection to a spiral staircase in the upper right corner of the drawing is considered by some to be evidence of its location, as this staircase seems to appear in other drawings of Villa Madama.

Yard without House

The project for the terraces is presented—in its unfinished form—as a bastard. Are they open squares or buildings? Villa Madama is characterized by a hillside location, and so the planning of the extensive grounds had to take into account the geographical conditions. The clearer the forms and the larger the individual elements of the garden and park were to be, the more drastic the measures on the terrain. In fact, the project of the three spaces is characterized by this requirement. Each of the three is defined in its junction to the next by long flights of stairs. The staircases do not appear as isolated elements, but are integrated into the boundaries of the square and follow its geometric form. Their length and number of steps—even if this still appears schematic—indicate large differences in height of approximately two stories between the individual levels. Now it becomes clear that the surfaces are bordered on one side by very high walls, which descend gradually on the adjoining two sides. In one sense, the surfaces can be read as architectural courtyards or forecourts, as it were, while in another, they open up a view of the landscape.

Stairs and Wall

Moving from one level to the next, the experience of spatial forms, scenographic situations, depends on where one looks. However, the elements that characterize this development are—and this drawing also makes it clear—not yet conclusively defined. Despite the radical reduction of the drawing, it reveals itself as a work in progress, a test of different solutions on one sheet. The circular surface is flanked by two variants for stairs, one of which lies outside the central geometries, in a gusset resulting from the approximation of square and circle. The second variant, probably of a later date, cuts into the surface of the square in the form shown, thus constituting an error. The drawing would have to be redone, with a square surface shifted by the width of the stairs. Then, however, the basic geometric forms would no longer touch each other directly. They would no longer be separated from each other by lines, but by surfaces or volumes. This problem has not yet been discussed. Its interest lies in the radical approach formulated by Raphael here, in which he himself has inscribed a kind of blurring.

Garden in the Landscape

Leaving behind this discussion of geometry, the project finally must be characterized by its content. As a garden in a landscape that, at the time, tended to be perceived as infinite, the project is conditioned by its clear boundaries. Let us make a contemporary comparison: the infinity pool with sea view, the swimming pool in the river, the swimming pool on the deck of a cruise ship. The similarity of substances—water here and there—is contrasted by the difference in access to the physically separated areas. In the appendix of *Delirious New York* (1978), Rem Koolhaas demonstrated the visionary possibilities of such a special situation. The Constructivists' raft, a swimming pool floating from New York to Europe, here stands for the uprising of pure optimism. The designed garden in the vastness of the (still) little-developed landscape can also be seen as an early precursor of such radical fantasies.

Projection

A similar geometrically pure form appears at another significant moment in Raphael's oeuvre. Just as this design for the terraces of the villa's gardens would not have lost, or should not have lost, its two-dimensional and conceptual origin if it had been realized in the spatial context of the landscape, a special element appears in some of Raphael's paintings: a kind of projection. It is inscribed in the image, defines its reading, but at the same time is completely removed from it—not integrated into the work, but placed on top of it. In the *Madonna Connestabile* (1502–4), *The Holy Family with the Lamb* (1504), or *Madonna del Granduca* (1505), to name but a few examples, the halo is the element that completes the work. It is painted last and placed onto the painting, remaining alien to it. We are here dealing with a radical concept, which is the origin of the work, creating content, life, and space in order to finally remain forever removed from all these developments.

fig. 01

fig. 02

fig. 03

fig. 04–05

fig.06–07

fig. 08–09

fig. 10–11

fig. 12

fig. 13-15

fig. 16-18

fig. 19

fig. 20–25

fig. 26

fig. 27–29

fig. 30–32

fig. 33–34

fig. 35–40

fig. 41–42

fig. 43–45

fig. 46–47

fig. 48

fig. 49

01 *Raphael Cartoons, Raphael Court, Victoria and Albert Museum, London, February 2020, n. 1*, London 2020.

02 *Giorgio Ghisi (printmaker), after Raphael, St. Paul in the School of Athens, print on paper, Accession number: DYCE.1280, Prints & Drawings Study Room, Victoria and Albert Museum, London*, London 2020.

03 *Raphael Cartoons, Raphael Court, Victoria and Albert Museum, London, February 2020, n. 2*, London 2020.

04 *Charles Thurston Thompson, Another View, View of packing case and horse-drawn 'van' for transport of Raphael Cartoons from Hampton Court to South Kensington Museum, 1865, Albumen print, Accession number: 44412, Prints & Drawings Study Room, Victoria and Albert Museum, London*, London 2020.

05 *Charles Thurston Thompson, Another View, View of packing case and horse-drawn 'van' for transport of Raphael Cartoons from Hampton Court to South Kensington Museum, 1865, Albumen print, Accession number: 44410, Prints & Drawings Study Room, Victoria and Albert Museum, London*, London 2020.

06 *Preparing the exhibition "Raffaello 1520-1483", Scuderie del Quirinale, Raffaello Sanzio, Ritratto di uomo, 1502-1504, oil on panel, 48 x 37 cm, Liechtenstein Museum, Inv.-No. GE36, Scuderie del Quirinale, Rome, n. 1*, Rome 2020.

07 *Preparing the exhibition "Raffaello 1520-1483", Scuderie del Quirinale, Raffaello Sanzio, Ritratto di uomo, 1502-1504, oil on panel, 48 x 37 cm, Liechtenstein Museum, Inv.-No. GE36, Scuderie del Quirinale, Rome, n. 2*, Rome 2020.

08 *Preparing the exhibition "Raffaello 1520-1483", Natalia Gurgone, Federica Mancini, Scuderie del Quirinale, Rome, n. 1*, Rome 2020.

09 *Preparing the exhibition "Raffaello 1520-1483", Natalia Gurgone, Federica Mancini, Scuderie del Quirinale, Rome, n. 2*, Rome 2020.

10 *Raffaello Sanzio, La muta, 1507, oil on panel, 64 x 48 cm, Galleria Nazionale delle Marche, Urbino, n. 1*, Urbino 2020. Courtesy: Galleria Nazionale delle Marche, MiC, Urbino.

11 *Raffaello Sanzio, La muta, 1507, oil on panel, 64 x 48 cm, Galleria Nazionale delle Marche, Urbino, n. 2*, Urbino 2020. Courtesy: Galleria Nazionale delle Marche, MiC, Urbino.

12 *Replica of the cartoon for The School of Athens, xerox prints in scale 1:2, Photography Studio, ISIA (Istituto Superiore per le Industrie Artistiche)*, Urbino 2020.

13 *Raphael's workshop, Loggia of Cupid and Psyche, 1518. Villa Farnesina, arch. Baldassarre Peruzzi, 1506-1511, Archivio Villa Farnesina, Rome, n. 1*, Rome 2020.

14 *Raphael's workshop, Loggia of Cupid and Psyche, Raphael Frescoes, Villa Farnesina, arch. Baldassarre Peruzzi, 1506-1511, Archivio Villa Farnesina, Rome, n. 3*, Rome 2020.

15 *Raphael's workshop, Loggia of Cupid and Psyche, Raphael Frescoes, Villa Farnesina, arch. Baldassarre Peruzzi, 1506-1511, Archivio Villa Farnesina, Rome, n. 2*, Rome 2020.

16 *Corner of Via della Longara with Salita del Buon Pastore, Rome, Scuderie Chigi, arch. Raffaello Sanzio, 1512-1514, n. 1*, Rome 2020.

17 *Corner of Via della Longara with Salita del Buon Pastore, Rome, Scuderie Chigi, arch. Raffaello Sanzio, 1512-1514, n. 2*, Rome 2020.

18 *Corner of Via della Longara with Salita del Buon Pastore, Rome, Scuderie Chigi, arch. Raffaello Sanzio, 1512-1514, n. 3*, Rome 2020.

19 *Medusa*, Trieste 2021.

20 *Chigi Chapel, arch. Raffaello Sanzio, before 1519, Santa Maria del Popolo, n. 1*, Rome 2020.

21 *Chigi Chapel, arch. Raffaello Sanzio, before 1519, Santa Maria del Popolo, n. 2*, Rome 2020.

22 *Chigi Chapel, arch. Raffaello Sanzio, before 1519, Santa Maria del Popolo, n. 3*, Rome 2020.

23 *Chigi Chapel, arch. Raffaello Sanzio, before 1519, Santa Maria del Popolo, n. 4*, Rome 2020.

24 *Chigi Chapel, arch. Raffaello Sanzio, before 1519, Santa Maria del Popolo, n. 5*, Rome 2020.

25 *Chigi Chapel, arch. Raffaello Sanzio, before 1519, Santa Maria del Popolo, n. 6*, Rome 2020.

26 *Via del Banco di Santo Spirito, Rome, Palazzo Alberini, arch. Raffaello Sanzio, 1515-1519*, Rome 2020.

27 *Looking inside the Pantheon, Rome, n. 1*, Rome 2020. Courtesy: Direzione Musei Statali della città di Roma - Pantheon.

28 *Looking inside the Pantheon, Rome, n. 2*, Rome 2020. Courtesy: Direzione Musei Statali della città di Roma - Pantheon.

29 *Looking inside the Pantheon, Rome, n. 3*, Rome 2020. Courtesy: Direzione Musei Statali della città di Roma - Pantheon.

30 *Jan van Tieghem and Frans Ghieteels (workshop), after Raphael, tapestries of the Acts of the Apostles, c. 1549-1557, wool and silk, Palazzo Ducale di Mantova, n. 1*, Mantua 2020.

31 *Jan van Tieghem and Frans Ghieteels (workshop), after Raphael, tapestries of the Acts of the Apostles, c. 1549-1557, wool and silk, Palazzo Ducale di Mantova, n. 2*, Mantua 2020.

32 *Jan van Tieghem and Frans Ghieteels (workshop), after Raphael, tapestries of the Acts of the Apostles, c. 1549-1557, wool and silk, Palazzo Ducale di Mantova, n. 3*, Mantua 2020.

33 *Città del Vaticano, Palazzo Pontificio, Cortile di S. Damaso, Loggia di Raffaello (secondo piano del porticato, braccio I), ottava campata, volta con Storie di Mosè, Roveto ardente e decorazioni a grottesche, negativo ai sali d'argento, 21 x 27 cm, n. D004148, Fondo Cugnoni, ICCD*, Rome 2020.

34 *Città del Vaticano, Palazzo Pontificio, Stanze di Raffaello, Stanza della Segnatura, particolare, negativo ai sali d'argento, 21 x 27 cm, n. D002342, Fondo Cugnoni, ICCD*, Rome 2020.

35 *Antonio da Sangallo il Giovane, Model of the Basilica di San Pietro, 1539-1546 (per gentile concessione della Fabbrica di San Pietro in Vaticano), San Girolamo Octagon, Basilica di San Pietro, Rome, n. 1*, Rome 2020.

36 *Antonio da Sangallo il Giovane, Model of the Basilica di San Pietro, 1539-1546 (per gentile concessione della Fabbrica di San Pietro in Vaticano), San Girolamo Octagon, Basilica di San Pietro, Rome, n. 2*, Rome 2020.

37 *Antonio da Sangallo il Giovane, Model of the Basilica di San Pietro, 1539-1546 (per gentile concessione della Fabbrica di San Pietro in Vaticano), San Girolamo Octagon, Basilica di San Pietro, Rome, n. 3*, Rome 2020.

38 *Antonio da Sangallo il Giovane, Model of the Basilica di San Pietro, 1539-1546 (per gentile concessione della Fabbrica di San Pietro in Vaticano), San Girolamo Octagon, Basilica di San Pietro, Rome, n. 4*, Rome 2020.

39 *Antonio da Sangallo il Giovane, Model of the Basilica di San Pietro, 1539-1546 (per gentile concessione della Fabbrica di San Pietro in Vaticano), San Girolamo Octagon, Basilica di San Pietro, Rome, n. 5*, Rome 2020.

40 *Antonio da Sangallo il Giovane, Model of the Basilica di San Pietro, 1539-1546 (per gentile concessione della Fabbrica di San Pietro in Vaticano), San Girolamo Octagon, Basilica di San Pietro, Rome, n. 6*, Rome 2020.

41 *Villa Madama, Loggia di Raffaello, Rome, arch. Raffaello Sanzio, 1520, Diptych n. 1*, Rome 2020.

42 *Villa Madama, Loggia di Raffaello, Rome, arch. Raffaello Sanzio, 1520, Diptych n. 1*, Rome 2020.

43 *Gardens of the Villa Madama, Rome, arch. Raffaello Sanzio, 1520, n. 1*, Rome 2020.

44 *Gardens of the Villa Madama, Rome, arch. Raffaello Sanzio, 1520, n. 2*, Rome 2020.

45 *Gardens of the Villa Madama, Rome, arch. Raffaello Sanzio, 1520, n. 3*, Rome 2020.

46 *Villa Madama, Loggia di Raffaello, Rome, arch. Raffaello Sanzio, 1520, Diptych n. 2*, Rome 2020.

47 *Villa Madama, Loggia di Raffaello, Rome, arch. Raffaello Sanzio, 1520, Diptych n. 2*, Rome 2020.

48 *Medusa*, Trieste 2021.

49 *Gardens of the Villa Madama, Rome, arch. Raffaello Sanzio, 1520, n. 4*, Rome 2020.

Stefano Graziani
Documents on Raphael

Project supported by the Directorate-General for Contemporary Creativity by the Italian Ministry of Culture under the Italian Council program (2019)

Directed by
Guido Beltramini, Stefano Graziani

Centro Internazionale di Studi di Architettura Andrea Palladio

In collaboration with
Atelier Kersten Geers, Accademia di Architettura, Università della Svizzera Italiana, Mendrisio
Fotogalleriet, Oslo
Sir John Soane's Museum, London
Stiftung Insel Hombroich, Neuss
Victoria and Albert Museum, London

Project supported by

italianCouncil
Bringing our Contemporary Art to the World

MiC Direzione Generale
Creatività Contemporanea

Research and general coordination
Marta Tonelli

Project management
Ilaria Abbondandolo (Palladio Museum)

Fifteen of the photographs presented in this volume were printed in a single edition and acquired for the collections of the Palladio Museum, Vicenza.

Inkjet prints
Mario Govino, Milan

Frames
Mauro Telò, Milan

We sincerely thank all those who made this project possible:
Carlo Birrozzi, Alessandro Coco, and Francesca Fabiani, Istituto Centrale per il Catalogo e la Documentazione, Rome
Stefano Brachetti, Luigi Gallo, and Marco Pierini, Galleria Nazionale delle Marche, Palazzo Ducale di Urbino
Serena Cinquegrana, Ministero degli Affari Esteri e della Cooperazione Internazionale
Carlo Colonna, Mario Giordana, Vitale Zanchettin, and Pietro Zander, Fabbrica di San Pietro in Vaticano, Rome
Ana Debenedetti, Sophy Thomas, Victoria and Albert Museum, London
Marco Delogu, Villa Madama, Rome
Lia Di Giacomo, Luca Mercuri, Pantheon, Rome
Anna Maria Guarino, Soprintendenza speciale archeologia belle arti e paesaggio, Rome
Natalia Gurgone, Matteo Lafranconi, Federica Mancini, and Flaminia Nardone, Scuderie del Quirinale, Rome
Stefano L'Occaso, Palazzo Ducale, Mantua
Virginia Lapenta, Villa Farnesina, Rome
Jonathan Pierini, Stefano Veschi, Istituto Superiore per le Industrie Artistiche, Urbino
Stefania Santini, Fondo Edifici di Culto, Chiesa di Santa Maria del Popolo, Rome
Aldo Vitali, Chiesa di Sant'Eligio degli Orefici, Rome

Thanks to
Maura K., Margherita G.

Stefano Graziani
Documents on Raphael

Edited by
Francesco Zanot

Centro Internazionale di Studi di Architettura Andrea Palladio

Texts
Guido Beltramini, Frank Boehm, Bruce Boucher, Pablo Bronstein, Antonio Cataldo, Emanuel Christ, Emanuele Coccia, Ana Debenedetti, Victoria Easton, Kersten Geers, Manuel Orazi, Maddalena Scimemi, Pier Paolo Tamburelli, Ellis Woodman, Francesco Zanot

Publishing editor
Ilaria Bombelli (Mousse)

Editorial coordination
Agnese Cantelmi (Mousse), Marta Tonelli

Proofreading
Agnese Cantelmi (Mousse), Lindsey Westbrook

Graphic design
Anna Azzali, Francesco Valtolina (Mousse)

Translations
English - Italian / Inglese - italiano
Ilaria Abbondandolo, Alice Montagnin
Italian - English / Italiano - inglese
Giuliana Racco
German - English / Tedesco - inglese
Elisa Calosi

Thanks to Claudia Miotti for the proofreading of Antonio Cataldo's text.

Published by
Mousse Publishing Contrappunto s.r.l.
Corso di Porta Romana 63, 20122, Milan
moussemagazine.it

Available through
Mousse Publishing, Milan
moussemagazine.it
DAP | Distributed Art Publishers, New York
artbook.com
Vice Versa Distribution, Berlin
Viceversaartbooks.com
Les presses du réel, Dijon
lespressesdureel.com
Antenna Books, London
antennabooks.com

First Edition
2021

Printed in Italy by
Grafiche Venziane, Venezia

ISBN 978-88-6749-460-6
27 € / 30 $

Photographic campaign authorized by:
Archivio fotografico del Fondo edifici di culto, Roma: 20-25
Archivio fotografico della Villa Farnesina, Roma: 13-15
Istituto Centrale per il Catalogo e la Documentazione - MiC: 33-34
Istituto Superiore per le Industrie Artistiche, Urbino: 12
Liechtenstein, The Princely Collections, Vaduz-Vienna: 6, 7
Ministero degli Affari Esteri e della Cooperazione Internazionale: 41-47, 49
Palazzo Ducale di Mantova - MiC: 30-32
Per gentile concessione del MiC - Galleria Nazionale delle Marche: 10, 11
Per gentile concessione della Direzione Musei Statali della Città di Roma - Pantheon: 27-29
Per gentile concessione della Fabbrica di San Pietro in Vaticano: cover, 35-40
Scuderie del Quirinale - MiC: 6-9
Victoria and Albert Museum, London: 1-5

FORNO

PIO · IX · PONT
OPTIMO · ET · MVNIFICENTISSIMO
VINDICI · ANTIQVITATIS
CELLAM · AREAMQ
PER · CAMILLVM · IACOBINVM
REDEMPTIS · AC · SOLO
TEMPLI · HVIVS · DECOR
VRBIS · ORNAMENTO
COLLEGIVM · ARCHEOLOG
MDCCCLIII

PIO · IX · PONT
OPTIMO · ET
QVOD · DOMIBVS
CELLAM · AREAMQ
PER · CAMILLVM · IACOBINVM
REDEMPTIS · AC · SOLO
TEMPLI · HVIVS
VRBIS · ORNAMENTO
COLLEGIVM
MDCCCLIII

PIO · IX · PONT
OPTIMO · ET
QVOD · DOMIBVS
CELLAM · AREAMQ
SINISTRORSVM · OCCVPANT
PER · CAMILLVM · IACOBINVM
REDEMPTIS · AC · SOLO
TEMPLI · HVIVS · DECORI
VRBIS · ORNAMENTO
COLLEGIVM
MDCCCLIII

Documents on Raphael
Stefano Graziani

A cura di Francesco Zanot

PALLADIO MUSEUM

Mousse Publishing

L’architetto fantasma e i suoi segugi
Guido Beltramini

Superopere
Francesco Zanot

I Cartoni di Raffaello per la Cappella Sistina al Victoria and Albert Museum
Ana Debenedetti

Ritratti obliqui
Ellis Woodman

Nulla sembra più fotografico o pittorico dell’amore
Emanuele Coccia

Drappi di velluto
Pablo Bronstein

Ipotesi sul passaggio delle nuvole nella *Scuola di Atene*
Pier Paolo Tamburelli

La Cappella Chigi di Raffaello: una lettura spaziale
Emanuel Christ

L’ossa con la carne, o lo spazio non è abbastanza
Victoria Easton

Luce dall’alto
Bruce Boucher

Grottesca
Manuel Orazi

Architettura romana
Kersten Geers

Lettera ai giovani
Antonio Cataldo

Nell’occhio della mente
Maddalena Scimemi

Le fantasie spaziali di Raffaello nel giardino di Villa Madama
Frank Boehm

L’architetto fantasma e i suoi segugi
Guido Beltramini

La mostra del 1984 in Campidoglio a Roma su *Raffaello architetto*, a cinquecentouno anni dalla sua nascita, fu il laboratorio dal quale un gruppo di storici dell’architettura uscì allo scoperto e impose una nuova visione della propria disciplina. Alla guida erano Howard Burns, Christoph Frommel, Pier Nicola Pagliara e Manfredo Tafuri. Guardavano loro le spalle i fratelli maggiori Arnaldo Bruschi, Christof Thoenes e soprattutto Jim Ackerman, che aveva aperto la strada con il suo *The Cortile del Belvedere* (1954).

I loro padri del primo dopoguerra avevano comunicato col pubblico attraverso grandi monografie che – a parte il capolavoro *The Architecture of Michelangelo* (1961) di Ackerman – costringevano a visioni in bianco e nero. Questa generazione voleva l’intera gamma dei grigi. La mostra fu importante perché costituì il momento pubblico in cui la storia dell’architettura cessò per sempre di essere solamente una storia delle forme e tipologie architettoniche, destinata ai professionisti in un eterno presente disciplinare, e fece invecchiare di colpo Bruno Zevi, Leonardo Benevolo e anche Vincent Scully.

Lo studio dell’architettura del passato fu portato nei contesti, divenne disciplina umanistica che intrecciava ideologie, religione, economia, mentalità sulla scorta della storia materiale degli *Annales* e degli studi di Carlo Ginzburg.

Al centro di questa nuova storia c’era il linguaggio dell’architettura, i suoi stilemi, le sue fonti, le sue genealogie. E il linguaggio portava con sé i disegni. Certamente i *survey drawings*, ma non più quelli delle scuole Beaux-Arts che restituivano la forma dell’edificio, bensì quelli che mutuavano le proprie tecniche dall’archeologia, per restituire la consistenza fisica dell’edificio, i suoi materiali e le sue fasi costruttive, leggendo la sua evoluzione nel tempo. In questo modo, un muro di maggior spessore poteva tradire una pre-esistenza medievale, che aveva condizionato le scelte del progetto successivo, oppure una tecnica o un materiale specifici potevano essere spie preziose per la cronologia delle parti, che consentivano di comprendere l’idea creativa originaria.

Al centro c’era soprattutto il disegno rinascimentale, guardato non più come immagine (come facevano gli storici dell’arte) ma come strumento con cui l’architetto concepiva e sviluppava il proprio progetto, e poi lo comunicava a clienti, maestranze e lettori. Ciò significava mettere a punto una nuova *scholarship* in grado di leggere i disegni architettonici, la loro autografia, la loro materialità: i fogli più interessanti diventarono i fogli di studio – dove le varianti si susseguivano e registravano anche i sentieri interrotti – e non più solo i *presentation drawings*, fogli rifiniti da mostrare ai committenti per sedurli, che avevano attratto per secoli i collezionisti. Anche di questi fogli diventavano importanti l’autografia, le cancellature; bisognava riconoscere le filigrane delle carte per poterle datare, i tipi di media dall’inchiostro, alla pietra rossa o nera. L’attenzione al disegno si completava con una attenzione del tutto nuova per il disegno di ricostruzione dei progetti non realizzati, per non fare solamente la storia dei vincitori, ovvero gli edifici costruiti. Il recupero, attraverso i disegni, di opere non costruite, segnò un passaggio fondamentale in quanto pose al centro la personalità creativa dell’architetto anziché le sue opere, considerando che in architettura – a differenza di scultura e pittura – spesso i progetti non realizzati rivelano caratteristiche sperimentali e anticipatrici. Una mostra di architettura come quella del 1984, così incentrata sui disegni, non sarebbe potuta succedere che in un momento in cui parallelamente, fra gli architetti praticanti, il PostModern ridava una centralità al disegno di architettura contemporaneo, usandolo come territorio privilegiato di ricerca (Aldo Rossi), conservandolo e esibendolo (nel 1984 apre il Deutsches Architekturmuseum di Francoforte).

La mostra del 1984 diede corpo ad un fantasma, Raffaello architetto, che ebbe un ruolo fondamentale nella invenzione dell’architettura del Rinascimento. All’ossatura degli ordini messa a punto da Bramante, Raffaello aggiunse la pelle e i nervi, reinventando il trattamento delle superfici. I suoi palazzi furono specchio della personalità del committente, resi riconoscibili sulla scena urbana come personaggi su un palcoscenico. Pianificò una campagna sistematica di rilievo archeologico delle rovine antiche. Definì teoricamente le modalità del disegno di architettura in pianta, prospetto e sezione, contrapposto alle rappresentazioni dei pittori. Sugli studi per la facciata di San Pietro si intrecciarono per la prima volta un ordine gigante ed un ordine minore, ma bisognerà attendere trent’anni, Michelangelo e Palladio per vederlo esistere nel mondo. Con Villa Madama reinventò la residenza in campagna, dando forma ad una tradizione che risaliva gli antichi romani. Eppure questo gigantesco contributo è stato quasi cancellato dalla storia. Palazzo Branconio dell’Aquila è stato demolito; palazzo da Brescia è stato smontato e rimontato in un sito incongruo; la chiesa di Sant’Eligio degli Orefici è stata modificata; Villa Madama è un meraviglioso frammento incompleto; le Stalle Chigi sono oggi dei ruderi; il progetto per San Pietro sopravvive solo nelle pagine del Codice Mellon a New York.

Poco prima che morisse, chiesero a Tafuri quale fosse la casa più bella del mondo. Rispose: “Una casa che non è mai stata costruita, la casa di Raffaello in via Giulia”.

Superopere
Francesco Zanot

Se Raffaello avesse avuto a disposizione la fotografia, molto probabilmente l’avrebbe utilizzata per compiere i suoi studi sui monumenti antichi. È infatti nota l’eccellenza dell’artista di Urbino non solo nei campi della pittura e dell’architettura, ma anche in quello archeologico, tanto da ricevere incarichi sullo studio delle vestigia romane da parte di Leone X e fondare buona parte del prestigio di cui godeva alla corte papale sulla “sua fama di sensibile conoscitore dell’antichità classica”.[1] In assenza di pellicole e obiettivi, Raffaello aveva affidato al disegno tecnico il compito di registrare le tracce del passato, organizzando autentiche campagne di rilevazione che ricordano esattamente il furore documentario dei decenni successivi alla nascita della fotografia. Qualche secolo più tardi, si sarebbe parlato di agenzie e corrispondenti per descrivere lo straordinario sforzo organizzativo che Vitruvio riferisce all’intuizione raffaellesca: “Era tanta la grandezza di questo huomo, che teneva disegnatori per tutta Italia, a Pozzuolo et fino in Grecia: né restò d’avere tutto quello, che di buono per questa arte potesse giovare”.[2]

L’opera fotografica realizzata da Stefano Graziani nel 2020 scaturisce proprio da questa intuizione; affonda le radici nella medesima terra di mezzo su cui si posava il programma di Raffaello, studioso del passato e, contemporaneamente, progettista del futuro. Nominato “Commissario delle Antichità” il 27 agosto del 1515 con il preciso scopo di evitare la distruzione dei marmi epigrafici, Raffaello immaginò una sequenza di azioni che andava ben oltre i termini della salvaguardia, a cui affiancò progetti di catalogazione, conservazione e, soprattutto, ricostruzione. Incluse inoltre le conoscenze storiche acquisite nella sua produzione artistica: tra gli esempi più noti ci sono l’arco d’accesso alla Cappella Chigi, evidente richiamo al portale del Pantheon, e le decorazioni di Villa Madama, ispirate ad alcuni motivi della Domus Aurea. Cinquecento anni più tardi, Graziani si intromette in questo dialogo e lo riattiva. Le sue fotografie riproducono solo apparentemente alcune opere raffaellesche: più precisamente sono immagini del loro rapporto/confronto con il tempo presente.

“Can you see the moon can you see it seen”,[3] scrisse Gertrude Stein un secolo fa in una frase che enfatizzava un aspetto rivoluzionario, quanto inevitabile, della natura stessa della fotografia. Ciò che è possibile vedere attraverso questo strumento, infatti, non è il soggetto stesso – la luna, che osserviamo alzando gli occhi al cielo –, ma una sua immagine filtrata attraverso lo sguardo di qualcuno che l’ha visto al posto nostro. Se questo è valido per qualsiasi fotografia, nel caso del lavoro di Graziani si tratta di un fondamentale oggetto d’indagine. Nel presentare una serie di opere d’arte, avvicinandoci al pensiero di un genio imprescindibile del Rinascimento italiano, Graziani misura il nostro distacco da loro. Siamo nel vasto campo della trasformazione. Carlo Mollino, architetto con un viscerale attaccamento alla fotografia, avrebbe piuttosto utilizzato il termine “trasfigurazione”, sottolineando la vena mistica di un processo che ha tuttavia radici molto concrete.[4] Nelle immagini di Graziani “ri-conosciamo” opere che nella realtà sono molto diverse: quadri, arazzi, architetture, sono tutti diventati fotografie. È il cardine della vitalità di questo medium, che anziché “immortalare” il proprio soggetto lo ravviva, mostrandone una prospettiva sempre inedita. Tutt’altro che inerti, le opere di Graziani offrono il piacere della sorpresa di scoprire qualcosa che è già stato scoperto. È una questione di circolarità (come ci ricorda Stein): sono opere di opere. In sintesi, portano all'estremo un criterio progettuale già utilizzato da Raffaello e già accennato qui sopra: la citazione. Se spesso si è parlato della fotografia come forma di appropriazione, rimarcandone il carattere unilaterale e predatorio, qui Graziani muta sensibilmente questo paradigma: la fonte è nota, oltre a offrirsi a una nuova interpretazione, il soggetto funziona da chiave di lettura per illuminare ciò che lo circonda, dentro e fuori l'inquadratura.

Nell'investigare la capacità trasformativa della fotografia, Graziani evidenzia parallelamente la natura alterata dei suoi soggetti. In pratica, nessuno di loro corrisponde all'opera che era apparsa agli occhi di Raffaello, ma si tratta in ogni caso dell'esito di differenti eventi e modificazioni succedutisi nel corso del tempo. Restauri, ristrutturazioni, ricostruzioni, realizzazioni ex novo sulla base dei progetti originali segnano la distanza tra passato e presente. Il sistema che l'artista urbinate aveva già in qualche modo considerato durante il suo impegno scientifico alle dipendenze vaticane rientra nuovamente in gioco. Graziani ne rappresenta la grande espansione in epoca contemporanea, fatta di luoghi (musei, università, archivi...), medium (tecnologie diagnostiche, materiali innovativi, display...) e persone (direttori, conservatori, registrar...). È un mastodontico, raffinato apparato formatosi per difendere un patrimonio economico e culturale. Questioni di potere si sovrappongono a imperativi etici che impongono di salvaguardare ciò che ancora possediamo per tramandarlo alle generazioni successive, consapevoli che esiste un limite alla possibilità di mantenere e replicare questa catena. Il realismo si scontra con l'utopia, risvegliando un'aspirazione, quella di rallentare o fermare il tempo, che percorre l'intera storia della speculazione umana, dalla tela di Penelope ai supereroi della Marvel. Secoli prima di Marcel Duchamp e Joseph Kosuth, Raffaello appare alla stregua di un artista concettuale, la cui idea prende il sopravvento sulla realizzazione. Con un'operazione uguale e contraria rispetto a quella eseguita da Walter Benjamin sul corpo della fotografia, Graziani mette in discussione l'aura delle opere che si trova davanti e verifica il rapporto che intrattengono con lo spettatore. Forse alcune pennellate sulla superficie di un affresco non sono scaturite da un gesto della mano di Raffaello, ma dalla perizia di un tecnico impegnato a rigenerare i colori come un algoritmo di Photoshop. Forse Raffaello non ha mai poggiato la schiena alla stessa parete dell'edificio che oggi questa sostiene. Graziani scardina certezze per fabbricare domande. Riprende il tema del rapporto tra originale e copia tanto caro alla storia dell'arte (da quando l'abitudine a collezionare ha moltiplicato le riproduzioni durante il periodo ellenistico) e a quella della fotografia. Soltanto che per Graziani originale e copia sono la stessa cosa. Opere individuali diventano il prodotto di un'enorme struttura, "superopere". Eppure corruttibili e delicatissime. La narrazione di Graziani oscilla paurosamente tra forza e fragilità. Così, anziché dedicare ad alcuni soggetti delle singole immagini, ne fa brevi serie composte da fotografie leggermente diverse tra loro, con un andamento quasi-cinematografico che ricorda la continuità orizzontale dei progetti raffaelleschi. Confrontandole, ciò che permane (resiste) emerge insieme a tutto quello che svanisce. Due termini opposti, appaiono qui straordinariamente somiglianti.

1 Christoph L. Frommel, "Raffaello e la sua carriera architettonica", in Frommel, Stefano Ray, Manfredo Tafuri (a cura di), *Raffaello architetto*, Electa, Milano 1984, p. 45.
2 Giorgic Vasari, *Le vite de' più eccellenti pittori, scultori e architettori*, Firenze 1550, p. 663.
3 Gertrude Stein, "A Circular Play" (1920), in Ulla E. Dydo, *A Stein Reader*, Northwestern University Press, Evanston 1993, p. 326-42.
4 Carlo Mollino, "I mezzi tecnico-fotografici di trasfigurazione estetica della natura", in *Il messaggio dalla camera oscura*, Chiantore, Torino 1949, p. 71.

I Cartoni di Raffaello per la Cappella Sistina al Victoria and Albert Museum

Ana Debenedetti

Nel 2020, per celebrare il quinto centenario della morte di Raffaello, il Victoria and Albert Museum (V&A) ha intrapreso un importante progetto di rinnovamento della cosiddetta Raphael Court (sala 48A), attuale collocazione dei sette cartoni superstiti che l'artista dipinse intorno al 1515-1516 per gli arazzi della Cappella Sistina (Palazzo Apostolico, Roma). Nel corso degli anni, lo status, il significato e la visibilità dei Cartoni hanno attraversato diverse fasi espositive e interpretative. Il nuovo allestimento valorizza, come mai prima d'ora, il nostro modo di guardare queste opere monumentali, permettendoci di considerarle quali tesori unici del Rinascimento, sia in termini di valore estetico che di risultato tecnico. I Cartoni raffigurano episodi chiave nella vita dei santi Pietro e Paolo; ognuno è composto da quasi duecento fogli di carta, per una dimensione complessiva compresa tra i 42-43 centimetri di altezza e i 28,5-29 centimetri di larghezza. Nell'estate del 2019 il V&A ha condotto una nuova campagna fotografica impiegando la pionieristica tecnica della scansione tridimensionale in combinazione con altri tipi d'indagine ottica, come la riflettografia infrarossa. A questo scopo, i vetri sono stati rimossi dalle cornici in modo da consentire ai curatori e ai conservatori di osservare da vicino non soltanto la straordinaria materialità di queste opere realizzate su carta – simile a una pelle d'elefante con le sue zone ruvide, le sue pieghe e i suoi strappi –, ma anche il genio estremamente poliedrico di Raffaello. La sua forza inventiva gli consentì non solo di adeguarsi al preesistente stile decorativo della cappella, ma anche di concepire una serie il cui tema iconografico era chiaramente collegato alle scene raffigurate sopra il registro inferiore, punto in cui gli arazzi dovevano essere appesi.

In questa occasione i Cartoni hanno rivelato anche l'eccezionale freschezza dei colori originali. Raffaello adoperò una tavolozza di colori freddi, acidi, in modo da legare cromaticamente le sue composizioni agli affreschi precedenti. Nel 1483 Perugino, Botticelli, Ghirlandaio e Signorelli, tra gli altri, completarono la prima fase del programma decorativo per papa Sisto IV (nato Francesco della Rovere, in carica dal 1471 al 1484) con scene della vita di Cristo e di Mosè. Un'ulteriore sfida per Raffaello fu quella di armonizzare i suoi dipinti con la volta da poco affrescata da Michelangelo, raffigurante scene dal Libro della Genesi con figure di sibille e profeti (1508-1512). La parete dell'altare, d'altro canto, conservava ancora l'affresco con l'Assunzione del Perugino, affiancata da due scene narrative che successivamente sarebbero state coperte dal *Giudizio universale* di Michelangelo (1536-1541). La riscoperta dei colori originali dei Cartoni ha restituito nuova vita alle composizioni; d'un tratto, tutti i personaggi appaiono impegnati in gesti vorticosi, con interazioni fra l'uno e l'altro, mentre l'intera serie sembra respirare, muoversi, reagire come un tutt'uno nonostante la sua incompletezza – tre dei Cartoni sono ancora perduti. Soltanto a questo punto si è compreso il ruolo e lo status effettivi di questi grandi dipinti, concepiti stilisticamente come basamento strutturale per le scene rappresentate al di sopra. Con le loro figure imponenti, disposte saldamente in primo piano, e il loro chiaro sviluppo narrativo, gli arazzi, derivati dai Cartoni, avrebbero accompagnato lo sguardo verso il livello superiore in un gioco di armonie cromatiche.

Realizzati da Raffaello e dalla sua bottega a velocità formidabile per una forma d'arte, quella dell'arazzo, con cui l'artista non aveva mai lavorato prima, i Cartoni furono immediatamente spediti a Bruxelles per essere filati nel laboratorio del mercante e tessitore Pieter van Aelst (1450-1533 circa). Da quel momento scomparvero alla vista del pubblico per quasi un secolo: se ne produssero dei duplicati da usare sui telai in quanto il processo di tessitura avrebbe danneggiato notevolmente i capolavori originali di Raffaello. Per la prima volta una serie di arazzi – tradizionalmente concepiti come beni mobili di lusso e con un grado di flessibilità tale da poterli sistemare in maniera di volta in volta diversa a seconda del luogo – era creata per un ambiente specifico. L'uso della prospettiva, la costruzione drammaturgica e compositiva nei dipinti di Raffaello aprirono una strada completamente nuova a questa forma d'arte. Considerate le diverse dimensioni delle scene, l'orientamento della luce (che si alterna da sinistra a destra) e la sequenza nell'ordine narrativo, si pensa che in origine queste opere fossero realizzate per una ben definita decorazione ad arazzo all'interno della Cappella Sistina. In che cosa potesse consistere la sequenza originale è ancora oggetto di discussione, ma è probabile che Raffaello avesse visto la prima esposizione degli arazzi nella Sistina – e potrebbe anche averne sovrinteso la messa in opera – quando sette di questi furono consegnati in Vaticano in tempo per la funzione di Santo Stefano del 1519. La sua morte prematura, nell'aprile del 1520, gli impedì di vedere la serie completa. I tre arazzi mancanti raggiunsero il Vaticano entro il dicembre 1521, poco prima della morte del papa. La scomparsa del loro artefice, seguita da quella del committente, probabilmente influì non poco sul destino degli stessi Cartoni che si ritennero perduti per quasi un secolo, fino a quando sette di loro riapparvero a Genova all'inizio del XVII secolo. Tuttavia, già nel 1521, uno di questi, *La Conversione di Saulo* (oggi scomparso), trovò il modo di tornare in Italia, dal momento che è documentato nell'importante collezione del cardinale Grimani (1461-1523) a Venezia.

Dall'inizio del XVI secolo si cominciarono a produrre sempre più cartoni *ben finiti*, generalmente monocromi, come disegni preparatori per affreschi e dipinti su cavalletto: alcuni venivano successivamente offerti a committenti importanti. Tale sviluppo coincise con l'emergere di un nuovo gusto per il collezionismo di opere su carta nella penisola e fuori dai confini italiani. È quindi probabile che tutti i Cartoni fossero destinati a entrare in collezioni prestigiose, o che dovessero essere restituiti al papa di modo tale da poter controllare la riproduzione oppure offrirli in dono; inoltre, se necessario, egli avrebbe potuto appenderli in sostituzione degli arazzi finiti, come era prassi in alcune chiese del Nord Europa. Invece, secondo la tradizione fu Pieter Paul Rubens a scoprirli a Genova all'inizio del 1600 e ad informare successivamente della loro esistenza il principe del Galles, futuro re Carlo I (in carica dal 1625 al 1649). I Cartoni furono acquisiti dalla Corona inglese nel 1623 specificamente come dipinti per l'arazzeria da poco fondata a Mortlake (allora un piccolo villaggio a ovest di Londra): lì si produssero nuovi duplicati, mentre i Cartoni stessi furono abbandonati in magazzino per altri ottant'anni. Fu soltanto sotto il regno di Guglielmo III (in carica dal 1682 al 1702) che i Cartoni riacquistarono a pieno titolo il loro status di opere d'arte. Nel palazzo di Hampton Court fu progettata una sala espositiva appositamente per loro, cosicché diventarono le uniche opere monumentali di Raffaello fuori dall'Italia. I Cartoni furono progressivamente riconosciuti tesori nazionali e giocarono un ruolo importante nella crescita di una consapevolezza storico-artistica in Gran Bretagna. Con l'avvento della regina Vittoria, nel 1837, e la successiva apertura al pubblico del palazzo di Hampton Court, i Cartoni divennero sempre più accessibili e alla metà del XIX secolo entrarono in una nuova fase della loro storia che li vide al centro di un'impresa ambiziosa ideata da Alberto, principe consorte della regina (1819-1861), nota come "Raphael Collection". La collezione comprendeva oltre 5.000 stampe e fotografie di ogni opera allora attribuita a Raffaello, o *da* Raffaello, al fine di mettere a disposizione degli studi sul maestro una risorsa visiva unica. La prematura scomparsa del principe consorte, nel dicembre 1861, impedì di vedere completato il suo progetto. Fu quindi in omaggio alla sua memoria che nel 1865 la regina accettò di prestare i Cartoni al South Kensington Museum (l'attuale V&A) da poco fondato, il cui programma culturale ed educativo era stato in parte ideato dallo stesso principe.

Oggi contemplare, osservare ed esaminare i Cartoni di Raffaello ci permette di riconciliare la loro funzione di dipinti per usi pratici con il loro status di capolavori assoluti, legati indissolubilmente al processo creativo di Raffaello. Realizzati per un ambiente e uno scopo specifici, gli immensi "affreschi tessuti" di Raffaello sono l'esempio di un'autentica rivoluzione nel disegno che, speriamo, continuerà a ispirare le generazioni future.

Ritratti obliqui
Ellis Woodman

Fra le collezioni del Victoria and Albert Museum (V&A) di Londra esiste una serie di negativi su lastra di vetro, ognuno dei quali ha le eroiche dimensioni di 3 piedi per lato (circa 1 metro quadrato) per 1/4 di pollice di spessore (circa 6 millimetri). I negativi furono realizzati nel 1858 dal primo fotografo interno all'istituzione, Charles Thurston Thompson, e documentano il ciclo dei sette Cartoni di Raffaello, allora conservato nel palazzo di Hampton Court, nella periferia occidentale della capitale britannica. In media ogni Cartone è largo 5 metri e alto 3,5 metri, fatto che rese impossibile fotografarli all'interno della sala che li ospitava. Nei giorni di bel tempo, i Cartoni furono quindi calati da una finestra in un cortile adiacente, consentendo a Thompson di fotografarli con la luce naturale e il supporto di una macchina fotografica di cui oggi non si conoscono le dimensioni, presumibilmente enormi. Dai negativi furono prodotte stampe all'albumina, che i conservatori annotarono per registrare con esattezza le condizioni fisiche dei Cartoni. Questa operazione costituì uno dei primi e più ambiziosi usi della fotografia per la documentazione di opere d'arte.

Come ha sostenuto Walter Benjamin nel suo famoso saggio del 1935, *L'opera d'arte nell'epoca della sua riproducibilità tecnica*, l'avvento della fotografia ha drasticamente ridotto il senso di autorevolezza, o "aura", tradizionalmente irradiato dalle opere d'arte. Eppure, il fatto che i Cartoni dovessero essere tra le prime immagini a sottoporsi al rischio di tale riproduzione non è privo d'ironia. Dopo tutto non erano mai stati concepiti come opere d'arte finali, ma come elaborati di progetto che avrebbero consentito la produzione di arazzi per mano di altri. I Cartoni, che raffigurano scene dei Vangeli e degli Atti degli Apostoli, furono realizzati da Raffaello e dalla sua bottega facendo uso di più fogli di carta incollati insieme su un supporto di tela, tra il 1515 e il 1516. Furono quindi inviati a Bruxelles dove l'atelier di Pieter van Aelst impiegò tre anni a tesserli, in tempo per la prima presentazione degli arazzi nella Cappella Sistina il giorno di Santo Stefano del 1519.

In realtà, quella fu solo la prima di una serie di versioni prodotte a partire dai Cartoni: sia Enrico VIII d'Inghilterra che Francesco I di Francia ne acquisirono delle serie. A partire dal 1516 erano stati utilizzati anche come base per la produzione di stampe, dimostrandosi particolarmente adatti a una loro reinterpretazione con questa tecnica perché Raffaello, sapendo che i suoi dipinti avrebbero dovuto funzionare efficacemente come arazzi, aveva privilegiato l'audacia degli effetti compositivi alla complessità dei dettagli. Fu principalmente attraverso la proliferazione delle stampe che le composizioni di Raffaello assunsero dunque una posizione centrale nell'immaginario culturale europeo.

Tuttavia, quando Thompson fotografa i Cartoni, la natura facilmente idealizzabile e riproducibile delle immagini di Raffaello aveva iniziato ad attirare notevoli critiche. Quando John Ruskin visitò Roma per la prima volta, nel 1840, annotò: "A Raffaello, in ogni modo, ho scoperto di non riuscire a dare alcun senso. L'unica cosa veramente chiara per me nelle sue composizioni era che tutti sembravano indicare tutti gli altri e che nessuno, a quanto ne sapevo, valeva la pena di essere indicato".[1] Gli affreschi del 1509-1511 nella Stanza della Segnatura, in Vaticano, furono motivo di particolare irritazione per il critico inglese. "Il declino del pensiero e dell'arte in Italia – scrisse Ruskin – risale a quel luogo e a quel tempo [...]. E fu determinato in gran parte dalle eccellenze stesse dell'uomo che aveva così segnato l'inizio del declino. La perfezione dell'esecuzione e la bellezza delle caratteristiche che furono raggiunte nelle sue opere e in quelle dei suoi grandi contemporanei, resero la finitura dell'esecuzione e la bellezza della forma gli obiettivi principali di tutti gli artisti; e da quel momento in poi si ricercò l'esecuzione piuttosto che il pensiero, e la bellezza piuttosto che la veridicità".[2]

La convinzione di Ruskin secondo cui le conquiste di Raffaello rappresentavano una fossilizzazione delle tendenze più vitali dell'arte medievale andava contro l'opinione della Royal Academy of Arts britannica, che stava energicamente promuovendo il maestro italiano come modello per una rinascita della pittura storica contemporanea. I Cartoni, che erano esposti al pubblico a Hampton Court, costituivano un elemento centrale di quella campagna. Le critiche di Ruskin nei confronti di Raffaello trovarono il robusto favore di una giovane generazione di artisti inglesi. Nel 1848, un gruppo di loro di cui facevano parte Wiliam Hollman Hunt, John Everett Millais e Dante Gabriel Rossetti fondò la Confraternita dei Preraffaelliti con il preciso scopo di riconnettere l'arte contemporanea a una tradizione che a loro avviso Raffaello aveva guastato. L'osservazione attenta della natura – e la sua rappresentazione con profusione di dettagli – divenne un principio cardine della lotta della Confraternita contro l'accademismo.

Nel 1865 Thompson realizzò un'ulteriore serie di fotografie, anch'essa conservata nella collezione del V&A, questa volta documentando una cassa da imballaggio trainata da cavalli, alta 6 metri, in cui i Cartoni sarebbero stati presto alloggiati. La regina Vittoria aveva da poco acconsentito a concedere il prestito a lungo termine dei Cartoni al nuovo museo intitolato a lei e al marito, e il contenitore su misura era stato fatto costruire per trasportarveli da Hampton Court. È l'elaborata struttura tecnica necessaria a garantire la conservazione di questi fragilissimi oggetti a catturare l'attenzione del fotografo. Paradossalmente, la decisione di non mostrare esplicitamente i Cartoni accresce la sensazione della loro presenza fisica.

I ritratti indiretti di Thompson risvegliano l'aura che la lunga storia delle loro riproduzioni aveva fatto tanto per offuscare.

1 E. T. Cook, Alexander Wedderburn (a cura di), *The Works of John Ruskin* (Library Edition), George Allen, Londra 1903-1912, Vol. 12, p. 148. Se non diversamente specificato, i testi originali resi qui in italiano sono curati dal traduttore.
2 *Ibid.*

Nulla sembra più fotografico o pittorico dell'amore
Emanuele Coccia

Nulla sembra più fotografico o pittorico dell'amore: nessun altro sentimento sembra essere connesso in maniera così intrinseca alla visione, nessun'altra relazione sembra nutrirsi e vivere di luce, di forme, di colori. Viceversa, è proprio in virtù di questa intimità con le forme e la visione che l'amore sembra essere così ossessivamente scelto come soggetto dalle arti visive e così legato alla loro storia. Se non è possibile amare senza poter immaginare – inteso come immergersi nell'immagine visiva dell'altro – ogni atto di immaginazione è un esercizio di amore. È per questo che nel *De Amore* di Andrea Cappellano, uno dei trattati medievali che influenzò per secoli la letteratura e la cultura europee, l'amore è definito come "una certa passione innata che procede dalla visione e dalla smoderata considerazione della forma dell'altro genere, a causa della quale qualcuno desidera sopra ogni cosa possedere gli amplessi dell'altro e che per volontà comune si possano realizzare in questi stessi amplessi i comandamenti dell'amore". Queste righe condensano l'esperienza moderna dell'amore e la poetica della modernità europea.

Il legame tra visione e amore è così profondo da renderci quasi impossibile riconoscere la sua contingenza. L'amore non è sempre stato la passione che nasce dalla visione. Nella versione che Apuleio ne fornisce nelle *Metamorfosi*, la favola di Amore e Psiche è un trattato sull'amore in quanto relazione e passione che non è accessibile attraverso le immagini e la visione. Questa strana forma di iconoclastia ritma e struttura il mito. È a causa della sua bellezza troppo visibile che Psyche non riesce a trovare amore: la si osserva come si osserva l'arte ("*mirantur quidem divinam speciem sed ut simulacrum fabre politum mirantur omnes*"). Una volta unita con Amore, lei scompare alla vista del resto degli uomini. Ma è nella relazione che l'assenza di visione diventa decisiva. La *forma mariti*, infatti, non è accessibile e ogni forma di desiderio di visione è bollata come curiosità sacrilega. L'unione si dà solo *praeter oculos*: solo attraverso il tatto e l'udito. Non si tratta solo di un divieto, ma di una impossibilità: una volta visto il volto di Amore, questo sarà costretto a sottrarsi per sempre dalla vista dell'amata. "Non vedrai più se avrai visto" ammonisce Amore a Psyche. L'amore di Psyche si costruisce come un atto di resistenza all'immagine negata ("*denegatae sacrosanctae imaginis tuae*"), una fedeltà a chi non ha volto, o la capacità di fare a meno del volto ("*Nec quicquam amplius in tuo vultu requiro*"). Infine, l'ultima prova che Psyche deve compiere, per conquistare il favore di Venere, è un'ennesimo divieto di visione: non guarda il contenuto di una scatola ("*hoc observandum praecipue tibi censeo, ne velis aperire vel inspicere illam quam feres pyxidem vel omnino divinae formonsitatis abditum curare curiosius thensaurum*").

Il cuore del racconto è in questo paradosso: la relazione con il dio Amore – *deus totius ignis*, dio di tutto il fuoco, quindi della luce – presuppone la fuga da ogni luce, o per dirlo con le parole di Apuleio è un rapporto "lucifugo", che ha orrore della luce. Grazie a questa natura "aniconica" l'amore può essere assimilato ad un mistero – nel senso religioso e cultuale del termine.

Il racconto di Apuleio non ha nulla di "mitologico", anzi sembra tradurre e rendere comprensibile, attraverso la narrazione, un'esperienza dell'amore molto più familiare e quotidiana di quella che l'ha identificato con un esercizio indisciplinato della visione. In questa sfera di esistenza amare significa sempre entrare in una relazione cultuale, liturgica con l'altro. La frequentazione e la condivisione ritmata e regolare di spazi e tempi comuni non ha luogo nella sfera cognitiva e non mira alla conoscenza dell'altro o dell'altra. L'amore si nutre del contatto e cerca l'intimità, non la conoscenza e l'identità. Amore è la capacità di prossimità a qualcuno di cui continua a sfuggirci il nome e il volto. Un esercizio di cecità volontaria e fedele a chi possiamo parlare e toccare ma non potremo mai vedere.

Dipingere questa esperienza erotica, come prova a fare il ciclo di affreschi di Raffaello nella loggia di Psyche, significa scontrarsi con un'impossibilità. Come poter dipingere la negazione dell'immagine dell'altro?

Se Raffaello prova a fare della pittura un corpo a corpo con i propri stessi limiti, l'esercizio a cui si presta Stefano Graziani fotografando il ciclo è ancora più vertiginoso. Non si tratta esclusivamente di trasformare un'opera pittorica – che deve mettere in scena un amore tattile e uditivo più che visivo e ottico – in visione fotografica, ma di iscrivere la relazione stessa tra fotografia e pittura nella sfera dell'amore aniconico. La fotografia non deve più riprodurre la visione pittorica: non c'è più competizione per chi riesce a conoscere meglio la realtà; non c'è più il tentativo di riprodurre l'esercizio pittorico secondo il massimo grado di fedeltà. Le pitture sono appena visibili. Ad essere messa in scena è solo l'intimità, la prossimità con l'immagine pittorica che sembra inaccessibile, proprio come il volto di Amore. La serie fotografica si sofferma sulla loggia, sulla sua atmosfera, come se dovesse suggerire la presenza dell'osservatore in quello spazio, più che ripetere con precisione l'esperienza visiva dell'opera di Raffaello. A uscirne trasformata non è tanto l'immagine o il senso dell'opera di Raffaello o il significato della sua arte ma la relazione tra il mezzo fotografico e la realtà. Di fronte a una tradizione che fa della fotografia una forma di "immoderata cogitatio" della realtà – un'immaginazione smodata e tutta visiva –, queste fotografie sembrano voler riattualizzare il programma di Apuleio dell'amore senza immagine.

Nell'opera di Graziani la fotografia diventa questo esercizio amorevole di cecità fedele e cultuale alla realtà. Non mira a scoprirne il volto o a fissarne l'identità. Non suscita l'amore per le cose, i luoghi, le persone, illuminandone i tratti. È qualcosa di più vicino a un appuntamento notturno con qualcuno o qualcosa di cui non si conosce il nome e di cui non sappiamo le origini. La macchina fotografica è un culto meccanico, ripetuto, liturgico per i corpi con cui continuiamo a scontrarci. È un modo per prometter loro che non abbiamo più bisogno del loro volto. La fotografia diventa un mistero: un modo per assicurarci quotidianamente che possiamo conoscere il mondo, letteralmente, anche senza i nostri occhi.

Drappi di velluto
Pablo Bronstein

Alcuni giovani si lasciano languidamente cadere su sedili di velluto. Certi posano con delicatezza l'esile mano sull'elsa dorata della spada che non sguaineranno mai. Altri reggono piccoli medaglioni delle loro amate volgendo appena lo sguardo all'osservatore, come a dire "no, vai tu a lavorare nei campi, io sono occupato".
Sebbene nell'Europa del XV e XVI secolo si assista a un revival della tradizione cavalleresca, che si manifesta nella popolarità di Ariosto o negli innumerevoli dipinti di San Giorgio che uccide il drago, a corte la galanteria restava qualcosa su cui spesso si doveva lavorare. Nel 1528 Baldassarre Castiglione (del quale Raffaello dipinse un ritratto) pubblicò *Il Cortegiano*, o *Il Libro del Cortegiano*. In quest'opera, concepita nel 1507 come un'informale conversazione semipubblica alla corte di Urbino, Castiglione insegna le buone maniere al cortigiano in erba. Le corti ducali erano spazi di socialità in cui spesso le persone mangiavano, defecavano e dormivano insieme in grandi stanze. Il modo in cui si apriva la porta a una signora poteva fare la differenza fra compiacere e infastidire qualcuno che era nella posizione di favorire o ostacolare l'ascesa sociale di chi compiva questo semplice gesto. Il libro si assicurava che il cortigiano fosse aggiornato sulle buone maniere non come serie di regole, ma come garbo personale con cui impressionare il principe presso cui si prestava servizio. L'enfasi era posta sulla spontaneità dei comportamenti, tale da creare un'aura di superiorità innata, una "eleganza" fisica frutto di una disposizione aperta e serena, di movimenti agili, delicati, e di un'aristocratica espressione del viso. La parola coniata per indicare questo fascino d'alta classe, apparentemente innato, è "sprezzatura".

Nel levigare gli spigoli e le asprezze infelici di un corpo "naturalmente" indisciplinato, la sprezzatura è come un'uniforme che nasconde i comportamenti irregolari, facendo ordine nell'individuo. Di sicuro l'individualismo non è sempre desiderabile, soprattutto se un cortigiano cerca di integrarsi e di mostrarsi a proprio agio. Dal momento che l'atteggiamento ricercato corrisponde a un gentile distacco, questo codice permette di fare passare inosservate le intenzioni recondite, proprio come accade a un ballerino classico quando nasconde lo sforzo fisico di un salto dietro a un'aggraziata curvatura della schiena. Perciò la sprezzatura non è soltanto un'uniforme, ma una maschera. Secondo il libro, il cortigiano dovrebbe dissimulare la fatica e, nel farlo, mascherare l'ambizione: "Perché dovrei preoccuparmi di tramare contro di te quando so a malapena chi sei?". All'epoca di Raffaello e Castiglione l'interprete della sprezzatura è un cortigiano "professionista", un aspirante rappresentante del loro stesso successo sociale, che occupa uno spazio intermedio, riconoscibilmente moderno, fra il mercante, il contadino e il principe.

Chi sono questi esseri superiori che popolano le scene sacre e filosofiche di Raffaello? Si tratta di figure ideali, e ciò che il libro del cortigiano cerca di instillare nel lettore è questo ideale. Ma lo strumento migliore per trasmettere la sprezzatura non sono i libri, bensì i quadri. I dipinti erano di grandi dimensioni, a colori e collocati in importanti ambienti della città, cosicché il loro impiego nella diffusione di gesti e pose assunse un'importanza fondamentale, comparabile al ruolo che hanno i film nell'influenzare il linguaggio attuale. Osservando i dipinti la gente poteva capire quali erano i gesti "buoni". Gesti legati al divino e al potere (la mano di Dio che crea Adamo, di Michelangelo), alla virtù e all'intelligenza (*La Scuola di Atene*, di Raffaello), alla raffinatezza e al fascino (le mani della *Monna Lisa*, di Leonardo). Oltretutto, è stata soltanto la generazione di Raffaello a restituire l'"eleganza" fisica in maniera convincente. Le Veneri e le Vergini di Botticelli o di Signorelli avevano una propensione all'eleganza, ma le loro dita non si erano ancora liberate dell'ossuta rigidezza tardomedievale. I dipinti stabilivano un punto d'arrivo per la posa, ovvero la posizione che si sarebbe dovuto riuscire ad assumere. Si tratta di un modello che non lascia spazio all'interpretazione, diversamente da quanto accade con il termine "raffinato" nel *Cortegiano*.

È divertente immaginare che la pittura abbia persuaso il pubblico a muoversi assumendo di tanto in tanto pose "famose". Tenendo le mani a metà tra la posizione di quelle di Adamo e della Monna Lisa, le persone potrebbero forse ritornare a un proto-elegante stato "di natura"? Oppure forse riescono a fondere ogni movimento in un flusso magmatico di sprezzatura? Raffaello dipinge il momento perfetto o persone perfette? Da un ritratto si può imparare a reclinare il capo in modo attraente, e senza dubbio qualunque tonto rinascimentale, per quanto goffo, sarebbe stato in grado di cavarsela. Ma come si allacciano le scarpe secondo la sprezzatura? Come si apre la porta a una signora? Se si solleva il braccio per tenere il polso in una particolare posizione che permetta di rilassare le dita e di allungarle elegantemente attorno alla maniglia della porta, cosa succede alla mano quando improvvisamente bisogna muovere il gomito e tirare? Come riuscirebbero i bifolchi a non attorcigliarsi nei più ridicoli grovigli? Cosa succederebbe se, mentre si è concentrati sull'eleganza delle braccia, non si notasse che i piedi sono piegati verso l'interno e le ginocchia si toccano mentre si cammina? Considerare il corpo nella sua interezza è qualcosa che sanno fare i ballerini o i mimi pratici dell'improvvisazione, ma è molto difficile per le persone comuni, tanto che la letteratura umoristica abbonda di cortigiani e paggi che inciampano sui propri piedi.

Lo sguardo sereno di quei giovani dagli occhi dolci rivela un'affascinante, malinconica, intima semplicità che appartiene loro fino dalla nascita; una esteriorità che è semplice riflesso di un'armonia interiore. Ma la sprezzatura può propagarsi dall'esterno verso l'interno? Se si seguono le istruzioni del libro facendo penzolare la gamba sinistra mollemente sopra la destra, i pensieri violenti lasciano il posto a un temperamento migliore? E se è così, tutti nella sprezzatura provano la stessa cosa? "Diventano" tutti la stessa "persona", proprio come i gentiluomini vittoriani la cui bombetta esprimeva sia lo status loro riconosciuto in società, sia una altrettanto accettata "decorosa" vita interiore? I personaggi di Raffaello appaiono effettivamente rilassati, intimamente ed esternamente, ma con l'avanzare del XVI secolo la sprezzatura fu sempre più adoperata dagli artisti per evocare situazioni emotive difficili. Artisti come Pontormo, Parmigianino e Rosso stravolgono i corpi oltre ogni verosimiglianza al fine di creare una sorta di iperbole emotiva. Gambe ridicolmente lunghe, torsi che ruotano di 180 gradi con apparente facilità, dita spaventosamente snodate, colli da giraffa che si avvitano nello spazio... Questi corpi non solo comunicano un'eleganza sovrumana suprema, ma permeano le immagini di una complicata tensione interiore. Andando contro al classicismo di Raffaello, questi corpi tesi, iper-eleganti, producono sull'osservatore un effetto di isteria.

Castiglione è preoccupato dalla femminilità troppo affettata di alcuni cortigiani. Con lo scopo di giungere a un comportamento ideale, c'è chiaramente il bisogno ci correggere questa tendenza da entrambe le parti. Da un lato ci sono rozzi teppisti provinciali che mangiano con le mani, dall'altro uomini che hanno preso a interessarsi un po' troppo alla compagnia reciproca, oltremodo consapevoli del proprio fascino, tanto da finire per ammorbidirsi troppo. Un compromesso con ogni probabilità vantaggioso fa sì che nei dipinti l'ambigua "checca" non prenda mai l'armatura per difendere la bella dama,e che allo stesso modo il mercenario zoticone non la faccia mai andare in estasi con lo strimpellio di un liuto sotto il pergolato. Sebbene, in realtà, molti di questi deboli, svenevoli personaggi che abbelliscono i ritratti manieristi, per i quali anche alzare una sola mano di Cristo durante la deposizione avrebbe costituito uno sforzo eccessivo, fossero di fatto violenti a livelli psicopatici.

Nei dipinti di Raffaello queste figure sono l'esempio di un perfetto bilanciamento tra eleganza e compostezza. I suoi uomini *contrapposti* sembrano vivaci più che annoiati, gentili ma non cedevoli, sfiorano il pavimento con delicatezza piuttosto che piroettare nello spazio. Ma in pittura la sprezzatura è un linguaggio di gesti transitori e di situazioni non definitive. Nonostante le pose possano esservi codificate, esse non hanno l'ultima parola su niente se non su loro stesse. La mano potrebbe indicare qualcosa, ma senza urgenza. Potrebbe brandire una spada, ma sappiamo che non la userà. A corte la sprezzatura deve aver rappresentato un linguaggio utile per stare seduti e conversare, quindi privo di significato per chi doveva svolgere lavori manuali. L'attenzione sulle mani, nella sprezzatura, implica che queste non debbano essere usate per lavorare la terra né per strofinare i vestiti. Ma è vero anche il contrario – che l'eleganza può essere raggiunta *solo* se non si è tenuti a fare quelle cose, o se il proprio lavoro consiste nel socializzare e il lavoro manuale è un'astrazione. Le corti che raggiungono il massimo livello di languida finezza, in cui la sprezzatura regna massimamente sovrana, sono "decadenti". Le corti di Versailles, di Carlo I, dei Romanov sono tutte stantie, paralizzate, e si preoccupano soltanto delle vicende interne e di acconciature. Corti che amano il balletto e le nappe, il trucco e il pettegolezzo, e che naturalmente sono piene di regine.

Ipotesi sul passaggio delle nuvole nella *Scuola di Atene*

Pier Paolo Tamburelli

Vasari scrive che Bramante "insegnò molte cose d'architettura a Raffaello da Urbino, e così gli ordinò i casamenti che poi tirò di prospettiva nella camera del Papa, dov'è il monte di Parnaso, nella qual camera Raffaello ritrasse Bramante che misura con certe seste".[1]

Non vedo motivo di dubitare di questa testimonianza estremamente circostanziata. Il racconto peraltro non dice che Bramante abbia disegnato di sua mano la scena di quella che oggi chiamiamo *Scuola di Atene* (1509-1511) e poi la abbia data bella e pronta a Raffaello. All'epoca, si stima nel 1509, Bramante "era vecchio e, dal parletico impedito le mani, non poteva come prima operare". Con tutta probabilità, non disegnava più. È più credibile che Bramante, ancora una volta "curatore" della scena artistica romana del primo Cinquecento, abbia semplicemente suggerito a Raffaello come affrontare il problema. E indubbiamente alcune caratteristiche dello "spettacolo di spazio" in cui camminano e dibattono i filosofi sono bramantesche: le pareti sono nude, senza troppa decorazione, l'edificio è tutto fatto di una materia unica ed uniforme, la sequenza di grandi navate coperte da volte a botte con lacunari, con pareti ritmate da piccoli scarti verso l'interno, produce una prospettiva che progressivamente si restringe, quasi misurando il tempo necessario a percorrerla. Le due volte più vicine all'osservatore sono intervallate da uno spazio più alto, che, a giudicare dalla sua luminosità, sarebbe da intendere più come un cortile a cielo aperto che come uno spazio cupolato, come si è quasi sempre fatto in omaggio all'idea che nell'architettura del Rinascimento debba comunque esserci una cupola. L'"edificio" che produce la scena della *Scuola di Atene* è un edificio "dipinto" e come tale va inteso, come una serie di quinte parallele, senza esigenze costruttive, a tratti anche piuttosto incoerente, fin troppo pieno di luce, senza coperture, se non i mezzi tubi delle volte a botte che connettono perpendicolarmente i vari piani del dipinto. Questo "edificio" è del tutto strumentale al dipinto e sacrifica sistematicamente la sua coerenza strutturale di architettura alla sua chiarezza visiva di dipinto, come è evidente nel dettaglio lucidamente sbagliato delle cornici "non inclinate" dei pilastri "non diagonali" su cui si dovrebbe impostare la "cupola" che non vediamo. Fin qui, tutti trucchi e scherzi e manie di Bramante, ma cosa aggiunge Raffaello?

Raffaello dipinge le nuvole. La scena della *Scuola di Atene* lascia tre porzioni di cielo dove piazzarle. Partendo dall'alto, una finestra con due colonne a livello del tamburo della (non) cupola, una lunetta compresa tra il margine inferiore della seconda volta a botte e il fregio dorico che conclude l'arco sullo sfondo e il passaggio al centro dell'arco, sopra le teste di Aristotele e Platone. Il cielo diventa più chiaro procedendo verso il basso, passando da un azzurro intenso dove le nuvole si stagliano nettamente ad un celeste sempre più pallido dove cielo e nuvole si confondono. Contando le nuvole, sempre dall'alto verso il basso, una velatura sfilacciata e bluastra si intravede a destra nella grande finestra del tamburo, un grande cumulo sodo e bianchissimo appare a sinistra nell'azzurro, sia sopra nella finestra che sotto la volta, un altro cumulo, più sfumato, è a destra, tagliato dal fregio a triglifi dell'arco, infine, sopra le teste di Platone e Aristotele degli stratocumuli più chiari che sfumano nel biancore del cielo in lontananza. L'elemento principale è la grande palla di vapore che spunta sopra nella finestra e sotto la volta, un'unica massa che il vento trasporta (certamente da sinistra a destra, anche se non saprei spiegare perché) verso il centro dell'immagine.

L'importanza del passaggio delle nuvole nella *Scuola di Atene* è provata dalla fissità della copia di Anton Raphael Mengs al Victoria and Albert Museum (1755), dove l'inquadratura rettangolare e il conseguente taglio orizzontale appena sotto i capitelli delle paraste in primo piano esclude tutta la prima volta a botte e la porzione superiore di cielo e finisce così per soffocare tutto lo "spettacolo di spazio" e soprattutto per escludere il passaggio delle nuvole. Mengs elimina la colonna d'aria sopra i filosofi e li schiaccia per terra, il suo cielo diventa tutto uguale. Lo spazio non si diffonde in profondità e non si espande più verso l'alto. Il gesto indirizzato verso l'alto di Platone sembra non avere più spazio in cui muoversi.

Infine cosa fanno le nuvole di Raffaello nello "spettacolo di spazio" di Bramante?

La macchina spaziale bramantesca è deliberatamente aperta sul cielo e volutamente costruita per reagire ai mutamenti del tempo, registrando i cambiamenti di luce, ma rimane tuttavia solo architettura, ferma, fissa, capace di rivolgersi al passaggio delle nuvole solo perché integralmente diversa. Raffaello occupa questo spazio immobile ed inanimato infilandoci sfacciatamente la vita che Bramante aveva avuto pudore di nominare. Le nuvole mostrano che lo spazio può essere usato, che è possibile pensarlo solo se se ne pensa anche un tempo, se si accetta che abbia una storia. Il passaggio delle nuvole è appunto la traccia minima di una storia, una storia ancora allo stadio embrionale di puro scorrere del tempo, di pura irripetibilità degli istanti. Il tempo passa; le nuvole si muovono, le loro configurazioni non si ripetono, non ci si può far passare due volte le stesse nuvole sulla testa. La storia, che Bramante vede sostanzialmente come un deposito di cose che possono essere riusate nel momento in cui tornassero utili, come "cava di citazioni"[2], per Raffaello è invece movimento e la possibilità di comprenderla è appunto la possibilità di intendere come alcune esperienze siano state possibili "in un preciso istante". Se per Bramante il collage di filosofi è un'astrazione che vive in una dimensione atemporale e non si deve preoccupare di mettersi in relazione con un vero evento, per Raffaello la *concordia Platonis et Aristotelis* è davvero possibile e quindi ha bisogno di incarnarsi in un momento storico reale, in un istante che possiede una specifica luce, in cui le nuvole si dispongono nel cielo in una configurazione che è irripetibile e proprio per questo *reale*. I sapienti che Bramante si accontenterebbe di elencare si devono invece incontrare nella realtà di un mattino sereno, devono appoggiare le natiche sugli scalini di marmo della loro scuola. La storia non è un magazzino di pezzi di ricambio, è un processo fatto di istanti ancor più concreti delle colossali tracce che lasciano nel paesaggio. L'interpretazione che Raffaello darà del lavoro di Bramante è già tutta qui, nell'alito di vento che passa nello "spettacolo di spazio".

1 Giorgio Vasari, *Le vite de' più eccellenti pittori, scultori ed architettori; con nuove annotazioni e commenti di Gaetano Milanesi. Tomo IV*, Sansoni, Firenze 1878, p. 159.

2 Gianfranco Contini, *Un'idea di Dante. Saggi danteschi*, Torino 1976, p. 75.

La Cappella Chigi di Raffaello: una lettura spaziale

Emanuel Christ

Costruire per immagini

Solo un pittore può costruire in questo modo. Tutto ciò che qui è fisicamente e vividamente presente in marmo e intonaco multicolore nasce dall'immaginazione pittorica, o forse piuttosto grafica, di un artista che vede l'architettura principalmente come motivo visivo: l'arco trionfale è innanzitutto un'immagine. Lo stesso vale per la forma circolare della cupola, per la piramide e persino per la pianta, una riproduzione di quella cruciforme di Bramante per la basilica di San Pietro. In altre parole, la Cappella Chigi a Santa Maria del Popolo di Raffaello è un'architettura composta da immagini e copie. Un'architettura pittorica che ciò nondimeno ha un effetto spaziale sbalorditivo, quasi illusorio, in un ambiente ridottissimo. Gli elementi più importanti di questa invenzione architettonica del pieno Rinascimento sono affrontati brevemente nei paragrafi che seguono.

La pianta: copia e incolla

Innanzitutto c'è la pianta. È composta da un quadrato ad angoli smussati (tali da renderlo in realtà un ottagono) con inscritto un cerchio. Svettanti ai quattro angoli, ognuno dei possenti sostegni angolari è a sua volta formato da due pilastri con in mezzo una nicchia, proprio come i piloni monumentali di San Pietro. Qui, se ancora non fossero abbastanza chiare, le origini della struttura architettonica di questa piccola cappella divengono evidenti. Raffaello si servì semplicemente di quanto aveva trovato in cantiere al Vaticano: come è ben noto, vi era giunto dopo Bramante, da pittore senza alcuna formazione architettonica. Senza tante cerimonie copiò la forma della struttura centrale ideata dal suo predecessore e la inserì nella basilica di Santa Maria del Popolo come una sorta di modello a scala ridotta (la cappella è almeno dieci volte più piccola della zona centrale del transetto di San Pietro). La notevole audacia di questa procedura di copia-e-incolla rivela che dietro al progetto non c'era soltanto una fervida immaginazione, ma anche molta ambizione: la piccola cappella compete con la più grande di tutte le chiese.

Questa idea non era comunque del tutto nuova: solo pochi anni prima, lo stesso Bramante – fra tutti – in certa misura aveva già proposto il tema del monumento in miniatura nel suo celebre Tempietto. Certamente non dev'essere stato facile per Raffaello: le parti interne delle chiese più piccole e più grandi di Roma erano già state disegnate dal suo predecessore. È chiaro che Raffaello avrebbe sempre potuto progettare solo o a imitazione di Bramante, o nel tentativo di distinguersi da lui (dopo tutto la sua architettura è assolutamente inconcepibile senza Bramante). Tuttavia, riuscì a inventare una nuova architettura completamente autonoma. Lo fece utilizzando i modelli bramanteschi (oltre a elementi tratti direttamente da immagini dell'antica Roma, naturalmente) e ricombinandoli tra loro in maniera sorprendente. O sarebbe forse più corretto dire che ne fece un collage e li pitturò?

La cupola: oltre la tettonica

Torniamo alla Cappella Chigi. Innalzandosi al di sopra della pianta equilatera, sostenuta da quattro archi a tutto sesto come a San Pietro, la cupola circolare poggia su un tamburo. La sua brillante finitura dorata è in forte contrasto con i materiali altrimenti piuttosto scuri della cappella, così per effetto del colore e della luce, la cupola sfonda lo spazio verso l'alto. Alziamo gli occhi a un cielo aureo scintillante di dipinti ed elementi architettonici. E al centro, la splendente calotta è aperta. Guardiamo direttamente dentro al paradiso (nonostante sia in gran parte celato da Dio). Come nel Pantheon, un'apertura circolare nella volta estende lo spazio architettonico all'infinito, anche se in questo caso si tratta di uno spazio dipinto. Questo gioco illusionistico fa sì che la nostra fiducia nel sistema tettonico dell'edificio vacilli per un momento; qui inoltre il soffitto stesso agisce in maniera alquanto anti-architettonica: intorno al medaglione, posto al centro della cupola, la struttura a cassettoni si addensa formando un'intelaiatura apparentemente solida simile a una crosta, che anziché sostenere sembra essere appesa. La volta assume la forma della cornice di un quadro: una soluzione impensabile per Bramante.

Quattro portali: l'illusione dello spazio aperto

Eppure, l'intervento pittorico più audace sta probabilmente nell'eliminazione delle tre pareti della cappella, poiché da un punto di vista architettonico sono solo i portali a delimitare lo spazio. Metaforicamente parlando, tutto il resto è aperto. L'effetto ottico della profondità è ottenuto ancora una volta usando colori e materiali a contrasto. Le paraste, le cornici e gli archi sono in marmo chiaro, quasi bianco. Tutto ciò che li separa – i rivestimenti murari, le nicchie e i rinfianchi –, al contrario, sono alternativamente di marmo nero e bruno oppure coperti da grandi tele scure. È questo a creare l'impressione della profondità spaziale. Anche il dipinto sulla parete centrale contribuisce al *trompe-l'oeil*. Guardando attraverso il portale (anch'esso copiato dal Pantheon) dalla navata, l'effetto è particolarmente dirompente. Riusciamo quasi a immaginare di essere davanti allo spazio completamente aperto della *Scuola di Atene* (1509-1511) prima dell'arrivo dei filosofi e dei pensatori.

La piramide: architettura iconica

Come se tutti questi abbinamenti e contrasti non suscitassero già abbastanza emozioni, a perfezionare la composizione visivo-spaziale una volta per tutte ci pensano due sarcofagi piramidali che occupano le pareti laterali. Qui Raffaello porta la sua concezione dello spazio all'estremo: è solo grazie a questi due oggetti che il muro retrostante assume un ruolo secondario e viene, in un certo senso, annullato. Le vere protagoniste dell'opera d'arte universale di questa cappellina sono le piramidi appuntite. Si tratta di una sorta d'invenzione iconica, l'eccezione nel sistema. Con la loro presenza quasi aggressiva, fanno esplodere la struttura architettonica. Come in un collage, si sovrappongono all'immagine in primo piano. Non solo nella forma, ma anche nel contenuto, queste sono l'esatto contrario dello spazio circolare creato da archi e volte. Nella tradizione classica la piramide (per esempio la Piramide Cestia) rimanda al regno dei morti negli inferi; eppure qui le piramidi non gravano neanche sul terreno come dovrebbero, anzi poggiano su sostegni rotondi e sembrano quasi galleggiare. Non serve grande fantasia per immaginare che presto si solleveranno dai loro piedistalli, i sarcofagi, per salire (come razzi) verso il cielo dorato. Difficilmente si può trovare un uso tanto anticonvenzionale della più grave di tutte le forme architettoniche. Forse solo il *Broken Obelisk* (1963-1967) di Barnett Newman costituisce una distorsione ancora più radicale di un monumento egizio.

Architettura metafisica?

Comunque sia, le piramidi richiamano alla mente anche un dipinto di Giorgio de Chirico conservato al Kunstmuseum di Basilea, dal titolo *L'énigme de la fatalité* (1914). La sua sagoma triangolare appuntita basta da sola a rendere memorabile questo famoso esempio di pittura metafisica. Il profilo del dipinto assomiglia in maniera incredibile a quello delle piramidi Chigi. L'associazione tuttavia non sta solo nella forma del dipinto, ma anche nel suo contenuto: circondata da archi, una stanza dal pavimento in lastre di pietra di due colori si apre verso il cielo. Un camino rosso occupa il centro della tela (al posto della Natività della Vergine). In primo piano, una mano rossa si allunga nello spazio dell'immagine, come fosse la mano di Gian Lorenzo Bernini che nel XVII secolo portò a termine la Cappella Chigi, mai conclusa da Raffaello, intervenendo sulla sua architettura con le proprie sculture. Un'incompiutezza che, in qualche modo, dura fino ad oggi, per via dell'ideale di apertura e d'incompletezza che ha portato con sé fin dal principio. L'architettura di Raffaello è più di quanto si riesca a vedere. In un certo senso, è metafisica: là dove termina lo spazio fisico dell'architettura ha inizio quello irreale della rappresentazione.

L'ossa con la carne, o lo spazio non è abbastanza

Victoria Easton

L'arte di Raffaello è stata riconosciuta "perfetta" sin dalle *Vite* di Giorgio Vasari, dove il biografo adopera questo termine almeno otto volte in riferimento all'opera dell'Urbinate. Vasari ne conclude "che invero noi abbiamo per lui l'arte, i colori e la invenzione unitamente ridotti a quella fine e perfezzione che appena si poteva sperare, né di passar lui già mai si pensi spirito alcuno",[1] come se nessun vocabolario disponesse di superlativi sufficienti a descrivere la maestria pittorica di Raffaello. L'idea di perfezione è intuitivamente comprensibile in relazione alla sua pittura che la maggior parte dei critici concorda avere raggiunto una sorta di apice che va oltre il concetto di bellezza.

In ogni caso, sarebbe possibile applicare lo stesso mantra della perfezione all'architettura di Raffaello? Questo è almeno ciò a cui Raffaello mira, come afferma in una lettera del 1514 allo zio – probabilmente il più citato dei pochi scritti di Raffaello – in cui indica come proprio mentore Fra Giocondo "ch'è uomo di gran riputazione sapientissimo, acciò ch'io possa imparare, se ha alcun bello secreto in architectura, acciò io diventa perfettissimo in quest'arte".[2] Di sicuro Raffaello si procura da sé i mezzi per commissionare una nuova traduzione di Vitruvio, che illustrerà personalmente (sapendo che, nel caso di Raffaello, *personalmente* significa per opera di alcuni dei suoi cinquanta disegnatori di bottega). Ma l'artista non si ferma qui e, quando viene designato soprintendente alle antichità di Roma, sviluppa un metodo estremamente accurato per rilevare le rovine, le quali non devono essere restituite come tali nel loro stato di abbandono, ma secondo il loro "progetto" originario. Raffaello è convinto della propria capacità di riportare in vita opere perdute in base alla sua interpretazione. Non si accontenta semplicemente di pianta e sezione. Lo spazio non è abbastanza, lui vuole l'involucro. Come lamenta l'artista, di Roma resta soltanto "la macchina del tutto, ma senza ornamenti, e – per dir così – l'ossa del corpo senza carne".[3]

Quasi nessuno di questi rilievi si è mai realmente concretizzato, cionondimeno la sua produzione architettonica "attribuita" testimonia l'entusiasmo di Raffaello nel volere riunire *tutto* – o almeno architettura, pittura e scultura – insieme: un *Gesamtkunstwerk* prima ancora che l'idea stessa fosse nata. O dovrei dire "Alles ist Architektur" (Tutto è architettura), come dichiarò nel 1967 Hans Hollein, uno dei pochi possibili *avatar* contemporanei di Raffaello. Hollein avrebbe sicuramente sognato di progettare la Cappella Chigi, dove l'opulenza delle forme, la ricchezza dei materiali e la pletora delle allegorie offuscano l'essenzialità della planimetria. La pianta Uffizi 165 A è probabilmente uno dei più bei disegni di Raffaello. Realizzato su carta quadrettata, è soltanto un semplice profilo che contorna una porzione vuota della pagina. Osservando questa sagoma, si intuisce lo stretto legame di Raffaello con Bramante, che progettò il coro della stessa chiesa, eccezionale per planarità, semplicità e utilizzo puro della luce come unica decorazione. Eppure, il contrasto con la cappella non potrebbe essere più impressionante, laddove Raffaello tenta di lasciarsi alle spalle la mancanza di decorazione e l'uniformità di materiali di Bramante. Bramante era solo ossa, Raffaello voleva la carne.[4]

L'origine dell'architettura sensuale di Raffaello si può fare risalire alla sua pratica di pittore. Nel XVI secolo avviene un forte cambiamento di paradigma in pittura quando la Madonna raffaellesca e il suo bambino "scendono dal loro piedistallo per essere travolti da vivaci gruppi di figure familiari che condividono la loro compagnia".[5] Nel dipinto "le figure non sono tanto composte all'interno dello spazio quanto riunite a dispetto di quello. Si guardano da vicino fissarsi ciecamente negli occhi e nella carne, afferrarsi, abbracciarsi e toccarsi il corpo l'una con l'altra come se il riconoscimento tra loro dipendesse molto più dal tatto che dalla vista".[6] In che termini questa discesa della Madonna in una sfera popolare – lontana da qualsiasi distanziamento sociale – diffusa intenzionalmente da Raffaello si riflette nella sua architettura?

Prendiamo per buone le parole di Raffaello e accettiamo che la carne dell'architettura sia la decorazione, che è uno dei suoi principali strumenti architettonici. Fin dalla teoria di Leon Battista Alberti, l'ornamento è considerato un'entità separata dalla struttura, ma d'altra parte non è un semplice riempimento. La decorazione è lo strumento con cui Raffaello può diventare un pittore di architettura e grazie al quale osa eludere le convenzioni con una scusa: *questo è solo ornamento*. Nella Loggia di Psiche, la vegetazione si trasforma in finte travature, in un intreccio di festoni vegetali – una sorta di ecologismo di facciata *ante litteram* – dove luce, colore, prospettiva e *trompe-l'oeil* insieme provocano un'esperienza immersiva, lasciando che il soffitto si dissolva nello spazio. La decorazione pittorica è più forte dell'architettura di Baldassarre Peruzzi, non soltanto come motivo ma perché riesce a legarsi allo spazio esterno del giardino e a diventare parte di un insieme più grande. Nella Cappella Chigi le pareti laterali sono impreziosite da scacchiere di due marmi diversi, che la coppia di disadorne e astratte piramidi copre brutalmente rompendo anche i limiti delle cornici. Ma nelle piramidi, invece di usare un marmo diverso, Raffaello ripropone lo stesso della griglia, confondendo la spazialità del geometrico intruso. L'effetto livellante del materiale contrasta con quello aggettante della piramide e dimostra allo stesso tempo maestria e ambiguità. La cappella è un oggetto completamente autonomo dalla chiesa, ma si è tentati di toccare la sua avvolgente *carnosità* come si accarezzerebbe la *Madonna* scesa fra noi.

Questa dissacrazione dello spazio si traduce in un'architettura molto inclusiva, di inaspettata generosità e che potrebbe sembrare "perfettamente compiuta". *Perfectio* significa letteralmente "compimento". Gli spazi di Raffaello sono effettivamente compiuti. Non vi è niente da aggiungere, né sollevano domande a cui rispondere, mettono tutti d'accordo. Ma di fronte a questa straordinaria e impareggiabile evidenza potremmo essere autorizzati a considerare l'opera architettonica di Raffaello, per dirla come Henri Focillon, "à la fois céleste et insignifiant".[7]

1 Giorgio Vasari, "Vita di Raffaello d'Urbino pittore et architetto", in *Le vite de' più eccellenti pittori, scultori e architettori*, Firenze 1568. Nelle sette occorrenze precedenti, Vasari scrive: "Dalle quali figure non potrebbe pittore alcuno formar cosa più leggiadra, né di maggior perfezzione", "… grandissima vivacità e colorito perfetto", "… un paese che in tutta perfezzione è singulare e bellissimo", "… con perfezzione non più da altri che da esso dipinta nella grazia del colorito…", "Il quale fece Raffaello finire con tanta perfezzione…", "… la quale egli di sua mano, continuamente lavorando, ridusse ad ultima perfezzione", "… tutt'e tre le Persone unitamente ristrette nella perfezzione dell'arte di Raffaello…", n.p.

2 Raffaello Sanzio, "Seconda lettera allo zio", 1514, in Ettore Camesasca (a cura di), *Raffaello Sanzio. Tutti gli scritti*, Rizzoli, Milano 1956.

3 Raffaello Sanzio, "Lettera a Leone X", 1519, in *Raffaello Sanzio. Tutti gli scritti*, n.p.

4 "Ché, avegna che a' dì nostri l'architectura sia molto svegliata e venuta assai proxima alla maniera delli antichi, come si vede per molte belle opere di Bramante, niente di meno li ornamenti non sono di materia tanto preziosa come li antichi, che con infinita spesa par che mettessero ad effetto ciò che imaginarno e che solo el volere rompesse ogni difficultate", *ibid*.

5 Robin Evans, " Figures, Doors and Passages", in *Translations from drawing to building and other essays*, Londra 2011 (prima ed. 1997), p. 54-90.

6 *Ibid*.

7 Henri Focillon, *Raphaël*, Edition Nilson, Parigi 1921, p. 12.

Luce dall'alto
Bruce Boucher

Esiste un disegno a penna e gessetto rosso di Raffaello raffigurante la cornice interna del Pantheon. È uno schizzo semplice, veloce, che coglie gli elementi essenziali delle modanature nel momento in cui catturano la luce dall'alto: deve trattarsi di uno dei tanti disegni di questa architettura iconica oggi non più esistenti. Il gessetto rosso dona lucentezza al profilo che aveva attratto l'occhio dell'artista e, anche a distanza di cinquecento anni, questa sembra irradiare dal foglio. Come tutti gli artisti del Rinascimento, Raffaello, nei suoi dipinti ma anche sulle facciate e negli ambienti interni di cappelle, ville e palazzi, era sensibile al modo in cui la luce colpisce le superfici. Si pensi ad esempio al bugnato gentile della facciata di palazzo Alberini a Roma, un richiamo a palazzo Caprini di Bramante – noto anche come Casa di Raffaello perché l'artista vi abitò nei suoi ultimi anni di vita. La luce del sole fa risaltare i motivi orizzontali e verticali che in assenza di un ordine architettonico canonico animano la facciata priva di colonne. La sua affinità con palazzo Caprini è visibile nel trattamento moderno delle botteghe e dei mezzanini al di sopra di esse; dal canto suo, il piano nobile appare elegante nel suo minimalismo con lesene al posto di un ordine di semicolonne.

Il solo torto che Giorgio Vasari fece a Raffaello fu quello di marginalizzare il suo lavoro di architetto nel proprio resoconto relativamente dettagliato della vita dell'artista pubblicato nelle *Vite*[1]. È opera di studiosi della seconda metà del XX secolo l'aver recuperato il senso della ricerca e dell'impegno che Raffaello profuse in questo campo. Se l'artista e papa Leone X de' Medici fossero vissuti più a lungo, Villa Madama e la nuova San Pietro avrebbero rappresentato il manifesto di uno stile "all'antica" più ricco, con una maggiore attenzione verso il colore e i dettagli decorativi, elementi che Raffaello trovava invece carenti nel modello bramantesco.

Naturalmente il Pantheon esercitava un grande fascino tanto sugli artisti quanto sugli antiquari, ma per Raffaello tale attrattiva si tradusse in un intenso periodo di studio e di assimilazione dei numerosi dettagli di quell'edificio tra gli altri dell'antica Roma allora in piedi. Lo si può vedere nella Cappella Chigi a Santa Maria del Popolo, un omaggio in miniatura al Pantheon in cui l'ambiente a pianta centrale coperto a cupola è impreziosito da marmi colorati, rilievi in bronzo, statue e mosaici. Raffaello era in stretti rapporti con il committente, il facoltoso Agostino Chigi: quest'ultimo sosteneva il tentativo dell'artista di ricreare i fasti dell'architettura classica, e dal canto suo Raffaello faceva tutto il possibile per riuscirvi. Qui la luce penetra dalla lanterna superiore, dando origine a una simbolica fonte di salvezza. Sebbene Raffaello avesse lasciato incompiuta la cappella, un secolo dopo Gian Lorenzo Bernini vi avrebbe riconosciuto con ragione un primo esempio di *Gesamtkunstwerk* o "opera d'arte totale", in cui tutti gli elementi erano subordinati alla visione del suo creatore. Le integrazioni di Bernini non solo completarono l'opera, ma svilupparono il modello raffaellesco in cui luce e colore sono modulati per diventare metafora dell'ascensione dello spirito.

Raffaello sperimentò idee simili in un altro progetto Chigi, la Farnesina, una villa realizzata da Baldassarre Peruzzi lungo le sponde del fiume a Trastevere. I suoi interventi si limitarono ad affreschi come il celebre Trionfo di Galatea (1512) e il *tour de force* della Loggia di Psiche (1518). Qui gli affreschi raccontano la leggenda di Amore e Psiche narrata dallo scrittore tardo romano Apuleio, in cui alla fine Psiche trionfa sulle persecuzioni di Venere. Raffaello concepì la loggia come una pergola a cielo aperto in cui i movimenti aerei degli dei si dispiegano sopra le nostre teste, con Mercurio che sembra volare da una parte all'altra dello spazio. In origine la sala era priva di vetrate, per cui aveva l'aspetto di uno spazio intermedio fra giardino e resto della villa, con cui forse s'intendeva evocare una macchina da festa per celebrare le nozze di Chigi e della sua sposa Francesca Ordeaschi.

La Roma papale concesse ampio spazio al grande talento di Raffaello pittore e architetto, ma uno dei suoi incarichi più importanti è probabilmente anche il meno conosciuto. Si tratta della serie di arazzi tessuti nelle Fiandre ma destinati a rivestire le pareti della Cappella Sistina. A commissionarla fu Leone X, ed entrambi – cliente e destinatario – destinarono agli arazzi un'attenzione speciale. Il papa oppose il genio di Raffaello a quello del suo più anziano rivale all'interno della Sistina; tuttavia, l'arte di progettare arazzi costituiva una novità per Raffaello e richiedeva un approccio diverso rispetto alla sua precedente attività di pittore. Gli arazzi erano destinati ad essere appesi sui settori inferiori delle pareti, sotto agli affreschi di fine Quattrocento con scene della vita di Mosè e di Gesù, a loro volta al di sotto del capolavoro di Michelangelo da poco terminato sul soffitto. I soggetti degli arazzi derivano dagli Atti degli Apostoli e completano la narrazione della volta che comincia dalla creazione del mondo e da Adamo ed Eva, prosegue con le storie di Mosè e di Cristo, per concludersi con la diffusione del Vangelo per opera di Pietro e Paolo. Gli arazzi di Raffaello erano allineati agli affreschi di carattere narrativo delle pareti soprastanti e, come questi, impreziositi da pannelli decorativi intermedi. Per ottenere l'effetto desiderato, Raffaello modificò il suo stile con figure più grandi e gesti più ampi, alla maniera di un moderno manifesto. Anche se lievemente sbiaditi dal tempo, i fili d'oro e d'argento degli arazzi brillano ancora, come hanno fatto lo scorso febbraio quando per un breve periodo sono stati riappesi nella Cappella Sistina per celebrare il quinto centenario della morte di Raffaello.

1 Giorgio Vasari, *Le vite de' più eccellenti pittori, scultori e architettori*, Firenze 1568.

Grottesca
Manuel Orazi

"Pictoribus atque poetis quidlibet audendi semper fuit aequa potestas".[1]

Nessun artista è stato dirimente come Raffaello e infatti la cultura tardoromantica ha fissato con il termine "preraffaellita" non solo e non tanto un aggettivo, ma un'autentica categoria dello spirito. Persino Alois Riegl, così refrattario alle singole individualità, lo ha scelto come spartiacque storiografico per la sua *Grammatica storica delle arti figurative* (2008). L'effetto dell'opera dell'urbinate non è solo postumo:

per misurare il suo impatto sui suoi contemporanei è sufficiente confrontare due opere di Lorenzo Lotto realizzate entrambe a Recanati. La distanza fra la prima, il *Polittico di San Domenico* (1508), e la seconda, *La trasfigurazione* (1512), è smisurata. Sembrano opere di due pittori diversi: la trepidazione stilistica del primo, dovuta forse alla sua religiosità cripto-protestante, è totalmente assente nella seconda, realizzata dopo il soggiorno romano del 1509 quando aveva lavorato a contatto diretto con Raffaello e gli altri artisti alla corte di Giulio II. Gli esasperati affreschi lotteschi non furono apprezzati dal papa guerriero, che era allora alla ricerca di un classicismo di stampo imperiale, di *instauratio urbis* e al contempo di *restitutio antiquitatis*, pertanto vennero cancellati e sostituiti proprio con quelli di Raffaello. Lo sbandamento del pittore veneziano, errante in quanto eretico, fu dunque definitivo – non tornerà mai più a Roma –, tanto che sulla via del ritorno verso le Marche si fermò in Umbria per vedere altre opere del Sanzio e del suo maestro Perugino, piegandosi quindi alla loro maniera per la *Trasfigurazione* recanatese, sebbene con qualche riluttanza.

L'opera architettonica di Raffaello si concentra invece nei suoi ultimi nove anni di vita (1511-1520) e anche se è difficile trovare una cifra unica per via della sua natura particolarmente corale, è possibile dire che mirasse non solo a "ritrovar le belle forme degli antichi", ma soprattutto alla "coincidenza tra Bello e Vero nella razionalità armonica della Regola"[2] nell'alveo di una generale sintesi delle arti. La compostezza delle sue figurazioni architettoniche, anticipate dalle architetture dipinte che fanno da sfondo alle prime opere come il tempio a pianta centrale nello *Sposalizio della Vergine* (1504) o all'invenzione della serliana nell'*Incendio di Borgo* (1514), è discorsiva e non assertiva come quella di Bramante, che forse era suo zio: "Apodittica, anche nel suo sperimentalismo, la lingua bramantesca; colloquiale quella raffaellesca".[3] La linea di condotta raffaellesca è dunque quella di una costante rielaborazione dei dati della romanità in termini di una variante d'autore, il che non escludeva citazioni di esperienze più recenti come la cupola coperta da un cono nella Cappella Chigi in Santa Maria del Popolo così come nel San Bernardino a Urbino di Francesco di Giorgio, "niente è più "Raffaello" di quella cupola" ha scritto Cesare Brandi.[4] Colloquiale, vale a dire profana e moderna, era la sua maniera di gestire le relazioni intellettuali, artistiche e professionali. Per niente sofferti erano i suoi scambi con i letterati come Baldassarre Castiglione, men che meno con i collaboratori, del tutto eccezionali, specie i pittori-architetti come lui: Giulio Romano e Baldassarre Peruzzi, che mai si piegarono difatti completamente alla maniera del maestro conservando le proprie inclinazioni. Altri, piuttosto, si specializzarono come Giovanni da Udine, virtuoso nel disegno degli animali e massimamente in quello delle grottesche, peraltro immediatamente diffuse nel gusto europeo grazie agli incisori fiamminghi – nelle Fiandre si realizzavano anche gli arazzi copiando i cartoni raffaelleschi. Secondo il giovane Manfredo Tafuri, il lavoro di Raffaello e della sua cerchia intorno alla sintesi delle arti è impostato soprattutto grazie all'ausilio della scoperta delle antiche "grottesche", un tipo di decorazione adeguato a un lavoro di gruppo e di rapida esecuzione. Tuttavia la calma olimpica del Sanzio e in ultima analisi il suo tanto decantato classicismo architettonico è stato perciò minato dallo strato più superficiale, cioè quello decorativo, presente tanto nella Farnesina quanto nelle logge vaticane e a Villa Madama: non a caso Vitruvio aveva condannato questo tipo onirico di ornato che causava, secondo André Chastel, la negazione dello spazio e la fusione delle specie, la mancanza di gravità delle forme e la proliferazione insolente di "ibridi". Da qui, dunque, emerge la contrapposizione classica fra la grazia cortigiana "voluttuosa e leggera" di Raffaello con la tragicità solitaria e forse nicodemista di Michelangelo, suo antagonista nella sintesi delle arti e in sprezzatura. È noto infatti il passo del letterato veneziano Lodovico Dolce (1557): "so ben io che in Roma, mentre che Raffaello viveva, la maggior parte, sì de' letterati, come de' periti dell'arte, lo anteponevano nella pittura a Michelangelo. E quelli, che inchinavano a Michelangelo, erano per lo più scultori: i quali si fermavano solamente sul disegno e sulla terribilità delle sue figure, parendo loro, che la maniera leggiadra e gentile di Raffaello fosse troppo facile, e per conseguenza non di tanto artificio: non sapendo che la facilità è il principale argomento della eccellenza di qualunque arte, e la più difficile a conseguire: ed è arte a nascondere la arte".[5]

Secondo Nikolaus Pevsner, il classicismo non corrisponde a uno stile preciso, come il gotico o il romanico, ma a un atteggiamento estetico; o forse si tratta di un'altra categoria dello spirito, quella propria di alcuni architetti nati negli anni Settanta (Dogma, Office KGDVS, 51N4E, LAN, Christ & Gantenbein, Baukuh et al.). Eppure le grandi personalità artistiche hanno fra le loro qualità anche l'enantiodromia e dunque al classicismo rinascimentale raffaellesco si oppone appunto il lavoro di gruppo nelle grottesche, figure proprie dell'Antirinascimento caratterizzate da un "miscuglio di rigore e inconsistenza che faceva pensare al sogno".[6] Non a caso Daniele Barbaro, mentore e mecenate dell'altro campione del classicismo che fu Palladio, nei suoi commentari vitruviani del 1556 le aveva già derubricate, e non a torto, *picturae somnium*: un sogno della pittura tanto deprecato dai classicisti rinascimentali quanto pregno di un infinito fascino inconsistente.

1 "Ai pittori e ai poeti è sempre stata concessa la giusta libertà di osare in ogni cosa", Orazio, *Ars poetica*, vv. 9.
2 Stefano Ray, "Il volo di Icaro. Raffaello, architettura e cultura", in Christoph L. Frommel, Stefano Ray, Manfredo Tafuri (a cura di), *Raffaello architetto*, Electa, Milano 1984, p. 57.
3 Manfredo Tafuri, "'Roma instaurata'. Strategie urbane e politiche pontificie nella Roma del primo Cinquecento", in *Raffaello architetto*, p. 63.
4 Cesare Brandi, *Disegno dell'architettura italiana*, Castelvecchi, Roma 2013, p. 196.
5 Ludovico Dolce, *L'Aretino. Dialogo della pittura*, Carabba, Lanciano 1913, p. 6-7.
6 André Chastel, *La grottesca*, Einaudi, Torino 1989, p. 17.

Architettura romana
Kersten Geers

Secondo Giorgio Vasari, Raffaello nacque a Urbino "in venerdì santo a ore tre di notte"[1] del 1483 e morì esattamente trentasette anni dopo, "il giorno medesimo che nacque, che fu il venerdì santo".[2] Con una coincidenza degna del suo divino talento, la sua morte sembrava parte di un piano preparato. L'improvvisa febbre alta, che si vociferava dipendesse da uno stile di vita fatto di eccessi, e il successivo salasso impropriamente praticato contribuirono alla prematura morte di Raffaello. Eppure, ebbe tempo (e potere, e amicizie) a sufficienza per disporre la propria sepoltura nel Pantheon, il monumento romano ribattezzato con il nome di Santa Maria Rotonda. In qualche modo, ciò si accordava esattamente alle licenze che, nell'arco della sua breve vita di artista e di architetto, Raffaello sembra avesse acquisito riguardo a tutto ciò che era romano, e per estensione raffaellesco.

Al tempo della morte di Raffaello, nel 1520, erano trascorsi solo sei anni dalla scomparsa di Bramante. Il gigantesco cantiere avviato da quest'ultimo in Vaticano con l'eliminazione dell'antica basilica di San Pietro era in corso da circa quindici anni. I cantieri di San Pietro e del Belvedere erano tutt'al più rovine, sia pure soggette alla dinamica inversa. Il grandioso progetto "romano" di Bramante, un tentativo di ricostruire il Vaticano secondo i principi degli Antichi, ebbe in qualche misura successo solamente per il caos che provocò. In quanto rovina immediata, che richiamava vagamente il Circo Massimo, questo risultava automaticamente romano. La morte del suo costruttore gli conferì un'aria d'inevitabilità storica, rafforzata dall'avvio dei lavori del Belvedere e dall'esecuzione dei quattro colossali pilastri della basilica di San Pietro. Le successive "versioni" di Raffaello, Baldassarre Peruzzi, Antonio da Sangallo il Giovane, e poi Michelangelo, oscillarono continuamente tra costruzione, ricostruzione, interpretazione e trasformazione, e quindi bene o male assicurarono in automatico la genealogia romana a qualsiasi esito. La maniera "all'antica" di Bramante era una questione concettuale, al cui centro stava il fatto di costruire *ex nihilo*. Imitando le tendenze imperiali e territoriali di Roma, questa si risolse in un'architettura astratta e semplice come conseguenza razionale a una circostanza forzata: l'architettura romana rappresentava il pragmatismo dopo la *tabula rasa*.

Dodici anni prima, nel 1508, Raffaello era giunto a Roma invitato da papa Giulio II, probabilmente su consiglio di Bramante, per dipingere un ciclo di affreschi negli appartamenti vaticani che si affacciavano sul cantiere del Belvedere. Al suo arrivo, Raffaello fece una serie di disegni del Pantheon, anche allora uno dei monumenti romani antichi più significativi. Uno dei disegni ha curiose particolarità. Parte suggestione spaziale, parte documento sintattico, presenta il monumento romano in maniera semplificata e netta ottenendo il massimo effetto plastico ed evocativo. Modificando gli ordini e accorciando la sequenza dei tabernacoli e dell'esedra, Raffaello ottiene un distillato di forme, varianti e peculiarità: un accumulo di elementi architettonici che vengono accuratamente corretti per mostrare l'idea architettonica del Pantheon. Dopo avere elencato le lievi ma significative differenze tra il Pantheon reale e quello idealizzato, tra l'edificio e il disegno, John Shearman scrive nel 1968: "l'unica spiegazione che posso dare è che sentiva che era meglio così".[3] Dal momento in cui mise piede a Roma, Raffaello cominciò a prendere posizione sull'architettura antica della Città Eterna, fondandosi su una raccolta erudita ma curata (e quindi selettiva) delle varianti antiche, come fosse un collezionista di sapere. Le sue conoscenze raggiunsero il culmine quando fu nominato soprintendente alle antichità di Roma e scrisse l'ormai famosa lettera a papa Leone X, sollecitando la protezione dell'architettura antica, ovvero di tutto quello che era sfuggito alla barbarie delle generazioni precedenti abituate a impiegare come materiale da costruzione qualunque cosa trovassero. Per conservare bisogna idealizzare, per idealizzare bisogna collezionare, con rigore e una buona dose di scienza, ma anche (e qui parafraso Shearman) con licenza. Anche se alla fine Raffaello sviluppò la propria architettura sulla base delle stesse ossessioni architettoniche della bottega di Bramante, sembra sia stato grazie all'adozione di licenze formali – la possibilità di interpretare e modificare una sintassi intrinseca a qualunque cosa antica studiasse – che fece sua l'architettura romana. Il disegno del Pantheon non è un'interpretazione scorretta o semplificata del Pantheon; è semplicemente il *suo* Pantheon.

Negli anni in cui lavorò sotto papa Leone X, la sua architettura si allargò a una scala più ampia. Per molti versi, Villa Madama, la cui costruzione iniziò nel 1519, è il Belvedere di Raffaello, sia per dimensioni, sia per ambizione. Costruita alla periferia di Roma, la villa doveva radunare ogni possibile variante romana in un unico gigantesco complesso edilizio, come una contemporanea Villa Adriana. Paradossalmente, forse come conseguenza diretta di una simile grandiosa ambizione, la costruzione si interruppe con la morte di Raffaello, miraggio di una romanità impossibile da raggiungere. Il Belvedere e la basilica di San Pietro, le impossibili rovine romane di Bramante, col tempo furono entrambi completati, fatto apparentemente inevitabile per via della loro imponente presenza e la chiara paternità. Col senno di poi, l'architettura di accumulo e appropriazione più sofisticata di Raffaello si rivelò anche la più vulnerabile, perché era intrinsecamente legata alla sua licenza (e a quella di Giulio Romano) e strettamente connessa alla maniera del suo autore. Quando l'autore morì, l'edificio scomparve. Il rovescio della tattica della paternità imposta, intrinseco all'atto di modificare, raccogliere e accumulare, richiede tempismo perfetto e azione immediata. Fu un'intuizione che Raffaello onorò sul letto di morte quando ordinò (e pagò) il restauro di uno degli antichi tabernacoli della Rotonda, in modo che potesse esservi sepolto. La curatela a volte richiede solo un nome. Il Pantheon è l'edificio più importante di Raffaello.

1 Giorgio Vasari, *Le vite de' più eccellenti pittori, scultori e architettori*, Firenze 1568, n. p.
2 *Ibid.*
3 John Shearman, *Journal of the Royal Society of Arts*, April 1968, Vol. 116, No. 5141, p. 401. Se non diversamente specificato, i testi originali resi qui in italiano sono curati dal traduttore.

Lettera ai giovani

Antonio Cataldo

Raffaello. I Musei Vaticani. Uno dei primi viaggi di studio nella capitale italiana che ho fatto da adolescente, accompagnato, con molta probabilità, da innumerevoli scombussolamenti ormonali, da altrettanti stati d'ebbrezza e ragazzate tipiche di quelle gite scolastiche. Ricordi giovanili che a ripensarci oggi sono molto meno personali di quello che credessi. La mia generazione. Mi sono reso conto col tempo di come tutti noi condividessimo gli stessi ricordi.

Una sorta di soggettività interconnessa formata dall'educazione ricevuta, dalle abitudini sociali, comprese quelle piccole scappatelle al di fuori delle rigide reti stabilite dalla società.

Noi, che abbiamo studiato arte come materia principale al liceo, abbiamo abbracciato senza mai mettere in discussione l'autorità estetica dello storico dell'arte Giulio Carlo Argan, il cui nome è stato onorato perché così avevano fatto anche i circoli accademici degli studenti prima di noi. Studenti che nella vita avevano compiuto passi che la maggior parte di noi non sarebbe mai riuscita a fare, per via delle condizioni sociali su cui poggiano le nostre origini e anche le nostre ovvie conseguenti aspirazioni. Noi eravamo, dopotutto, studenti di piccole città di provincia, cresciuti in famiglie lavoratrici, per lo più precarie e a basso reddito – del tipo idealizzato da intellettuali dell'alta società come Pier Paolo Pasolini in quanto appartenenti a esistenze evanescenti. Senza volerlo, siamo invece rimasti imbrigliati in una condizione che si ripete all'infinito, quasi fosse l'effetto del rimbalzare dei riflessi tra due specchi paralleli.

Noi non eravamo nelle stesse condizioni, né avevamo gli stessi contatti di Argan. E non eravamo di Torino, la prima capitale d'Italia che, come osservato da Antonio Gramsci, sotto il re Vittorio Emanuele II, portò al Sud diverse forme di colonizzazione e di esproprio.

Argan dal canto suo si unì ai ranghi del Partito Fascista nel 1928 (proprio mentre Gramsci fu imprigionato dal regime e non sopravvisse) e da prodigio qual era ottenne molti incarichi prestigiosi. Dopo la guerra passò, come tanti intellettuali, al PCI (Partito Comunista Italiano). Fu assolto dai suoi peccati politici dal leader del partito Palmiro Togliatti senza dover fare la minima penitenza. Molti anni dopo, nel 1968 Argan scrisse la *Storia dell'arte italiana*, da noi considerata la "bibbia di storia dell'arte". Per questa ragione lo conosco. Di sicuro tra le pagine di quel libro ho visto per la prima volta e imparato ad apprezzare l'opera di Raffaello.

Raffaello, colui "che più chiaramente pone l'arte come fine a se stessa o, quanto meno, come attività che non può attingere alle sue finalità ultime se prima non si realizzi e giustifichi come arte".[1] Lo stesso libro sottolinea che gli anni di Raffaello a Roma sono centrali per la definizione del Classicismo quale "sereno possesso di una concezione unitaria del mondo".[2] L'ambizione di catturare entro un'unica ideologia l'onnicomprensivo mondo conosciuto, a dispetto del numero di vite che è costato costruirlo, canonizzarlo, evangelizzarlo, è un credo perverso. È questo probabilmente il motivo per cui, in quanto studenti del popolo, ci è stato insegnato a distinguere tra l'"uomo" e l'"intellettuale", tra l'opera d'arte e la vita dell'artista. Oggi, dopo tutti questi anni, mi rendo conto di quanto tale separazione fosse cruciale affinché così tanti fatti trovassero giustificazione. Era in questa spaccatura tra il personaggio e la rappresentazione che si riuscivano a proclamare certi dogmi e a liquidare domande imprescindibili sulla vita degli uomini di fama (e infami).

Oggi vorrei chiedere: Raffaello non era a conoscenza della violenta opera di evangelizzazione della Chiesa e di quanto essa si spingesse lontano? Non era a conoscenza dell'approvazione di Cristoforo Colombo da parte della Chiesa? Non era consapevole del genocidio, di un numero di persone fra i 55 e i 100 milioni, che la conquista delle Americhe da parte di Colombo avrebbe portato con sé? Non era a conoscenza di questi fatti quando, nel 1509, dipinse il ritratto di Colombo che fu appeso a fianco di altri uomini "illustri" in Vaticano? Non sapeva che le sue rappresentazioni contribuivano a costruire una nuova visione del mondo – un mondo i cui confini si allargavano sotto ai suoi occhi ma la cui concezione doveva essere sancita entro un unico ideale, quello della Chiesa?

Giulio II, soprannominato il "papa guerriero" e noto come il maggiore mecenate delle arti della stirpe papale[3], lanciò un programma edilizio su vasta scala che costituiva, allo stesso tempo, una restaurazione economica, politica e ideologica[4]. La *renovatio* era un modello di cittadinanza (*civitas*) più "perfetta" di fronte a una realtà di conflitti, rivalità e crisi religiose e politiche. Il 21 dicembre 1507, festa di San Tommaso, Egidio da Viterbo, portavoce di Giulio II, pronunciò una lunga orazione nella basilica di San Pietro. Giulio II aveva ricevuto dal re Manuele I del Portogallo notizie gloriose sulle zone dei suoi interessi commerciali in Estremo Oriente, che comprendevano Ceylon (Sri Lanka), Calicut (Kozhikode) e il Madagascar. Non a caso le celebrazioni sono avvenute proprio quel giorno: lo stesso San Tommaso si dice avesse convertito i cristiani siriaci in India, e questo intreccio con la narrazione biblica permise a Giulio II di dimostrare un "ininterrotto Impero cristiano della fede" che portava a un ordine mondiale completamente nuovo, guidato dalla sua concezione.[5] La *renovatio urbis*, edificazione morale di un commercio, una bellezza e una legalità ai massimi livelli, sta alla base della cultura artistica e umanistica di Giulio II. Raffaello sembra essere stato determinante per l'affermazione di questi ideali e, allo stesso tempo, essersi rimesso ad essi. L'arte di Raffaello racchiude il contingente e il trascendente entro un'unità immediatamente comprensibile e, secondo Argan, destinata a diventare e rimanere popolare. Era l'arte ufficiale della Chiesa in un'epoca in cui "difendere l'evidenza della rivelazione contro l'ansia del problema religioso" era di fondamentale importanza.[6]

Quando Raffaello, al culmine della sua fama, ritrasse Giulio II – in quello che è considerato un importante punto di svolta in quel genere di ritratti per il rilievo dato al profilo psicologico del soggetto – non sapeva che avrebbe "umanizzato", e quindi "giustificato", quel personaggio, quasi come una vittima della sua stessa umanità?

La critica d'arte Carla Lonzi, che contesta l'approccio "eterodirezionale" e iperprivilegiato di Argan, intende smantellare questo tipo di posizioni guidate dall'ideologia.[7] Il critico, secondo Lonzi, deve attribuire alla "personalità storica [...] il rischio degli artisti, [...] le stesse interne ragioni".[8] Lonzi esprime dissenso nei confronti della critica accademica e della sua indebita contiguità tra "vita" e "ideologia".[9] Secondo lei, la critica d'arte accademica è per molti versi inaffidabile. L'attività critica può sopravvivere solo come testimonianza, attraverso livelli argomentativi che intreccino memoria personale e indagine storica[10]. La metterei in questi termini: interrogare e muoversi tra una soggettività collettiva data, un'identità soggettiva e la soggettività stessa.

La riproducibilità delle immagini ha contribuito a favorire ulteriormente l'amore quotidiano per il potere e l'ideologia, e una loro capillare distribuzione, laddove la fotografia era determinante per costruire mitologie. È in questa ripetizione, nella costruzione di una cultura di massa priva di prospettiva critica, che Raffaello diventa più importante per ciò che rappresenta come personaggio e come eroe costruito che non per il contenuto della sua opera. È qui, nell'essere testimoni dell'indulgenza della sua opera in quanto tale, che troviamo la tipica lezione per rovesciare il paradigma sull'*arte in sé* che Argan aveva cercato di fissare. L'arte in sé, in quanto dogma della Chiesa cattolica, si realizza nella sua vuota ripetizione, senza bisogno di spiegazioni; il potere del dogma risiede nel mantenerlo indiscusso ogni singolo giorno, letteralmente senza cercare un'altra angolazione, un altro punto della storia a noi ancora sconosciuto. È il senso letterale della fotografia contro quello della ripetizione, l'essere testimoni contro il documento, il quotidiano contro la storia, oggi contro ieri.

1 Giulio Carlo Argan, *Storia dell'arte italiana*, Sansoni, Firenze 1968, p. 428.

2 Ivi, p. 427.

3 Massimo Rospocher, *Il papa guerriero. Giulio II nello spazio pubblico europeo*, Società editrice il Mulino, Bologna 2015.

4 Tale ristrutturazione urbana è allo stesso tempo una riorganizzazione economica, politica e ideologica, basata sui piani urbanistici di Niccolò V e Sisto IV. Roma tornò a essere il motore amministrativo e finanziario di quanto accadeva nelle diverse province direttamente o indirettamente soggette all'autorità pontificia, assumendo una propria fisionomia, anche in termini di sviluppo urbanistico, di città capitale. Sulla collocazione della città di Roma nel contesto della struttura generale dello Stato pontificio, sui suoi valori simbolici e sulle trasformazioni che incidono sul suo sviluppo urbano si vedano i saggi contenuti in Luigi Salerno, Luigi Spezzaferro, Manfredo Tafuri (a cura di), *Via Giulia. Una utopia urbanistica del '500*, Staderini, Roma 1973; e Manfredo Tafuri, "'Roma instaurata'. Strategie urbane e politiche pontificie nella Roma del primo Cinquecento", in Christoph L. Frommel, Stefano Ray, Manfredo Tafuri (a cura di), *Raffaello architetto*, Electa, Milano 1984, p. 59-106.

5 "Non ci resta che riconoscere ciò che il re Manuele del Portogallo ha donato a questi popoli [dell'India e di Ceylon] nel recare loro i rami dell'albero [di Giulio II]... Manuele, conquistatore di Ceylon e del Golfo del Bengala, è incoronato da foglie di quercia, perché insieme alla quercia d'oro reca loro un'età dell'oro". Francis X. Martin, *Friar, Reformer, and Renaissance Scholar. Life and Work of Giles of Viterbo, 1469-1532*, Villanova 1992, cit. in Nicholas Temple, *Renovatio Urbis: Giles of Viterbo and the 'Golden Age' of Julius II*: https://www.academia.edu/37077006/Renovatio_Urbis_Giles_of_Viterbo_and_the_Golden_Age_of_Julius_II
Se non diversamente specificato, i testi originali resi qui in italiano sono curati dal traduttore.

6 "Compito dell'artista, dunque, non è di correggere la sembianza illusoria, ma di rendere manifesta, dimostrare la verità delle sembianze. È proprio per questa unità di contingente e trascendente nella solare evidenza della forma che l'arte di Raffaello è stata immediatamente capita, è diventata subito, ed è rimasta, popolare; ed ha rappresentato l'arte ufficiale della Chiesa". Argan, *Storia dell'arte italiana,* p. 447.

7 Carla Lonzi, "Jean Fautrier, la pittura informale e la '*chose vue*'", *L'approdo letterario*, V, 5, gennaio-marzo 1959, p. 136-138. Su questo e sui successivi contributi di Carla Lonzi citati, cfr. anche Michele Dantini, "Una polemica situata e da situare. Dicembre 1963: Lonzi vs Argan", in Flavio Fergonzi, Francesco Tedeschi (a cura di), *Arte italiana 1960-1964. Identità culturale, confronti internazionali, modelli americani*, Electa, Milano 2017, p. 105-120: 108.

8 Carla Lonzi, "Michel Tapié e la mostra *Strutture e stile* al Museo d'Arte Moderna di Torino", *L'approdo letterario*, VIII, 19, luglio-settembre 1962, p. 159.

9 Carla Lonzi, "Mostra della critica italiana 1961", *L'approdo letterario*, VIII, 17-18, gennaio-giugno 1962, p. 214-215.

10 Carla Lonzi, "Solitudine di un critico", *Avanti!*, 13 dicembre 1963, p. 23.

Nell'occhio della mente

Maddalena Scimemi

Otto fogli manoscritti dell'Archivio di Stato di Firenze, privi di autore e di intestazione, traducono in parole il progetto della grandiosa residenza alle porte di Roma voluta da papa Leone X. Una villa all'antica, destinata al cardinale Giulio de' Medici e collocata sulle falde di Monte Mario: il suo cantiere, avviato nell'estate del 1518, impegnerà Raffaello nell'ultimo, intenso anno di vita. Solo nella primavera del 1522 verrà utilizzata una prima volta, e ciò avverrà senza Raffaello e senza il pontefice, venuto a mancare pochi mesi prima.

La datazione del documento oscilla tra l'inverno del 1518 e quello del 1519, ed è opinione condivisa che si tratti di una copia da un originale di Raffaello, passata per le mani di Baldassarre Castiglione perché il letterato mantovano vi apponga delle integrazioni. L'ecfrasi della villa, ispirata alle descrizioni delle ville di Plinio il Giovane nelle sue Epistole, è frutto di scelte sofisticate e ponderate. L'estensore adotta termini latini e li volgarizza, segue una precisa gerarchia nel descrivere i diversi ambienti aperti e chiusi, adduce sempre le ragioni che determinano la loro posizione e la forma, chiarendo la geometria e la misura di ciascuno spazio. Il lettore è rapito dal suo racconto, che possiede una forte componente cinematica: riga dopo riga si ha la sensazione di visitare la villa al suo braccio, di esser condotti da un cortile a un interno, poi di nuovo a un giardino, e di seguito di rientrare, cambiare sala e seguire la luce spingendoci sino al parapetto di una loggia, per affacciarci sul vuoto e contemplare il fiume, i prati e Roma. Se non suonasse anacronistico, verrebbe da pensare che le sue parole mirano a simulare un'esperienza filmica *ante litteram*. Si tratta di una fonte documentaria la cui interpretazione non è lineare; una fonte preziosa che agisce alla stregua di una rete di fili dorati, nella quale sono impigliati diversi personaggi, collegati eventi, intrecciati significati. Poiché nella realtà disponiamo soltanto di un frammento di Villa Madama lasciato incompleto dal 1527, il documento costituisce una fonte imprescindibile per comprendere il progetto nella sua interezza.

Al momento della stesura della "lettera", se si accetta la datazione più precoce, l'architettura non è ancora distinguibile, ma qualcosa si può intuire. Alla fine del 1518, infatti, si sta procedendo a livellare i terrazzamenti del terreno a disposizione, dolcemente digradante sino alle sponde del Tevere. I lavori sono cominciati nel punto in cui è prevista una grande peschiera, coordinando i movimenti di terra con lo scavo della vasca e delle canalizzazioni, erigendo sostruzioni e muri di fondazione. È questo un cantiere strategico affinché il papa possa disporre – prima di qualunque altro spazio – di una terrazza panoramica dove poter banchettare all'aperto con i suoi ospiti, allietati da giochi d'acqua, da sculture di divinità antiche e da animali esotici.

La terrazza con la peschiera, rivolta all'"oriente equinoziale" per meglio godere dei venti favorevoli e dei raggi del sole, trae profitto dalla topografia di Monte Mario. Posta ad un livello inferiore rispetto a quello degli appartamenti, raggiungibile con una scala aperta e collegata a una cucina segreta, verrà addossata a un muro di sostruzione lungo e profondo, scavato da tre nicchie percorribili grazie a un passaggio aperto nello spessore dei contrafforti. Sebastiano Serlio loderà a parole nel IV Libro del *Trattato di Architettura* (1573) l'efficacia della soluzione strutturale, e di Andrea Palladio esiste nelle collezioni del RIBA (Royal Institute of British Architects) un prezioso disegno dedicato a Villa Madama in cui il terrazzamento è tracciato in pianta e in alzato.

Torniamo alla lettera, nella quale la descrizione relativa alla terrazza si risolve in un passo veloce, se lo confrontiamo con altre parti in cui abbondano particolari: "Et infine della scala volta a Maestro ha a lato l'acqua una cenatione, molto delectevole et per il fresco et per la veduta". Bastano poche parole per quello che probabilmente, già nell'inverno 1518, è il punto più leggibile dell'intero cantiere. Il testo riporta una "cenatione", una camera da pranzo all'aperto, ad una quota più bassa (come effettivamente è), ma la colloca all'estremità nord della vasca, ovvero più distante dalla villa di quanto non sia in realtà.

La velocità del passaggio della descrizione verbale e la nuova collocazione più comoda, dal punto di vista funzionale, sono dunque indizi che raccontano di un impianto definito ma elastico, nel quale gli aggiustamenti sono determinati da considerazioni innanzitutto di ordine pratico, in grado di mantenere la logica dell'impianto (un luogo appartato ma panoramico, fresco, con una vasca e giochi d'acqua) riconfigurandone la forma.

Allo stesso tempo, la posizione eccentrica della "cenazione", descritta dalla lettera e poi abbandonata, identifica un preciso istante della genesi del progetto nel quale, come in un lampo, possiamo scorgere l'intersezione tra la profonda comprensione dell'Antico in Raffaello e la fantasia delle sue invenzioni. Nella corrispondenza di Pietro Bembo è noto il passo in cui l'umanista veneziano annuncia, nella primavera del 1516, una gita di gentiluomini in compagnia di Raffaello per visitare le antichità di Tivoli. Passeranno trent'anni prima che Pirro Ligorio, architetto e archeologo napoletano, identifichi Adriano come committente del complesso e riconosca nelle rovine poste all'estremità di una lunga valle il tempio del dio Canopo, adornato di marmi e di giochi d'acqua. Ma nulla esclude che – già nel secondo decennio del Cinquecento, quando ancora la conoscenza archeologica della villa era a uno stato aurorale – quelle rovine viste da Raffaello l'abbiano stimolato a "inventare" il triclinio all'aperto e nella sua prima posizione, all'estremo opposto del terrazzamento rispetto alla villa.

Se nel caso della "cenatione" possiamo contare sul confronto con la soluzione realizzata, un altro passo della lettera risulta cruciale per comprendere l'importanza di quello che in realtà non verrà mai costruito e che, se ci si limita a considerare quanto è disegnato nelle due piante conservate agli Uffizi (GDSU 273 A *recto* e GDSU 314 A *recto*), può apparire come un dettaglio marginale.

Nella calibrata sequenza che sottende la descrizione della lettera, la prima architettura scelta per introdurre la descrizione dell'intero complesso è quella di un torrione tondo, che dona "bellezza et superbia" all'entrata, eretto nel punto più esposto del sito a mezza costa della montagna. Sembra di sentirsi addosso, leggendo, il soffio del "grecho", il vento freddo e secco che in certe giornate terse viene da nord est.

Sopra al torrione, del diametro di sei canne, la lettera descrive un ambiente tondo, tutto finestrato. È un luogo appartato, posto nell'angolo estremo di un giardino che profuma di aranci ("melangholi") ed è allietato dal gorgoglio di una fontana che prende acqua dalla "viva vena". Lo stesso giardino è uno spazio isolato dalla sontuosa sequenza di cortili e di appartamenti della villa, malgrado sia collocato a ridosso dell'entrata principale: a monte un alto muro ne impedisce la vista a chi percorre i "lochi pubblici", mentre a valle è protetto da un "andito" stretto e lungo, un passaggio coperto che termina proprio nel torrione angolare.

Anche se il torrione serve "anchora a uno poco de difesa", in realtà è un piccolo padiglione, uno spazio "piacevolissimo a starvi": i raggi bassi del sole invernale, col passare delle ore, toccheranno una dopo l'altra le aperture "invetriate", che girando "intorno intorno… traspaiono", lasciando vedere Roma a mezzodì, e a oriente i dolci meandri del Tevere. Il padiglione è definito "dyeta […] alegrissima" per la luce e per la vista. Esistono precedenti antichi di ville turrite: sono le residenze affacciate sulla costa tirrenica dell'*Ager cosano*, un territorio ben noto a Raffaello e ai suoi collaboratori di fronte all'Argentario. Ma nessun torricino di queste ville antiche può ospitare uno spazio vivibile al suo interno. Nella lettera, invece, si descrivono un giardino pensile con un parapetto affacciato sul paesaggio e un corridoio con all'estremità questo ibrido torrione/*dieta*, che evoca e distilla le esperienze dei palazzi di Urbino, Pienza, delle ville di Fiesole, e persino di un precedente romano, qual è il piccolo ambiente posto in angolo al *Viridarium* del palazzo di Venezia.

È in questo spazio, che ha le proporzioni di un piccolo casino (il diametro supera di poco i 6 metri), che si ragionerà tra gentiluomini nella stagione più fredda, la lettera lo annuncia strategicamente. Volendo tradurlo nel lessico moderno, potremmo definirlo un piccolo belvedere, un *gate lodge*, una sorta di *fumoir ante litteram*. Immaginarne gli ospiti, ancora oggi, non è difficile: sono i protagonisti di una élite immortalata nei ritratti di Raffaello, primi fra tutti il pontefice e il suo ambasciatore, Giulio de' Medici, e poi lo stesso Castiglione, il segretario Bembo, il datario Baldassarre Turini e i cardinali più legati alla corte medicea. Sembra incredibile che, potendo scegliere tra il cortile circolare, un atrio vitruviano, il teatro all'aperto, la loggia estiva, persino delle piccole terme e ovviamente la "cenatione", il conversare tra gentiluomini sia riferito a questo piccolo ambiente isolato, ancorché dalla vista spettacolare. Eppure questa scelta rappresenta un perfetto ritratto di Raffaello architetto.

Anche senza il costruito – come nel caso della "dieta invernale" che si comprende solo perché descritta nella lettera – la scintilla dell'invenzione di Raffaello continua a brillare oltre il documento.

Le fantasie spaziali di Raffaello nel giardino di Villa Madama

Frank Boehm

Frammento e fantasia

Sebbene Villa Madama – come si presenta oggi – sia un edificio imponente, questa è soltanto parte di un progetto più ampio che non fu mai portato a termine. Questo progetto incompiuto ha catturato l'immaginazione per secoli. Il suo eccezionale fascino deriva dalla totale mancanza di elementi costitutivi. Poiché la costruzione fu completata solo a metà, oggi al posto della corte rotonda che era stata progettata al suo interno troviamo un imprevisto cortile semicircolare. Le strutture all'aperto, pensate come ampliamenti della casa, sono in gran parte assenti. Ciononostante, si è detto che Villa Madama è uno dei pochissimi edifici moderni di Roma di cui Andrea Palladio abbia fatto un disegno in scala. Che effetto spaziale avrebbe avuto un edificio realizzato per intero nella cornice di quel grande parco?

Il disegno come manifesto

Il contributo di Raffaello all'architettura è ben noto, eppure è messo largamente in ombra dalla sua fama di pittore e disegnatore.[1] I suoi progetti architettonici o non sono stati realizzati, oppure sono stati costruiti solo per frammenti, rielaborati o distrutti da altri. Anche i disegni dei suoi progetti d'architettura sono rari e di solito noti attraverso altre fonti. In sostanza, mancano i riferimenti. Fa eccezione il disegno di progetto per le terrazze dei giardini di Villa Madama del 1518 circa, conservato al Gabinetto Disegni e Stampe delle Gallerie degli Uffizi (inv. 1356 A *recto*). L'unico disegno del complesso attribuito con certezza a Raffaello non riguarda la villa in sé, ma un settore dell'esterno. A fronte della sua dedizione all'antico, che espresse nella lettera a Leone X del 1519, questo disegno è di un radicalismo completamente autonomo.

Pura geometria

Il disegno mostra la pianta del piano terreno di una sequenza di tre ambienti, per lo più senza elementi di contesto. Un quadrato nella parte superiore è seguito da un cerchio al centro e, sotto a questo, da un'ellisse con i due fuochi a una distanza tale da corrispondere esattamente al diametro della circonferenza. A differenza dei cortili che si aprono all'interno della volumetria dell'edificio, nel disegno questi spazi, limitati solo da muri, spingono l'uno contro l'altro. I contorni delle figure geometriche semplici sono tangenti fra loro e la composizione tripartita è estremamente ridotta. Se si considera che il complesso non doveva probabilmente essere costruito in collegamento spaziale diretto con la villa – la ricerca non è unanime riguardo la sua collocazione precisa[2] – ma doveva proiettarsi sul paesaggio circostante, la coerenza del linguaggio formale diventa evidente. Posto sull'ambiente naturale – un'idea di appropriazione di origine urbana –, il puro quadrato subisce quindi un'evoluzione spaziale e si trasforma in un cerchio, che a sua volta muta in un'ellisse, cioè un quadrato allungato da due semicerchi. Godendosi il parco della villa, un visitatore assisterebbe a una lezione di geometria.

Giardino senza casa

Il progetto delle terrazze si presenta – nella sua forma incompiuta – come un ibrido. Si tratta di piazzali aperti o di edifici? Caratteristica di Villa Madama è la posizione sul fianco di una collina: la progettazione del parco doveva tenere conto della situazione geografica. Quanto più chiare saranno le forme e quanto più grandi i singoli elementi del giardino e del parco, tanto più drastiche saranno le misure sul terreno. In effetti, il progetto dei tre spazi è definito sulla base di questa esigenza. Ciascuno dei tre, in corrispondenza del collegamento con l'ambiente successivo, è delimitato da lunghe rampe di scale. Le scale non appaiono come elementi isolati, ma sono integrate nelle linee di confine dei piazzali, ovvero ne seguono la forma geometrica. La loro lunghezza e il numero di gradini – anche se questo risulta ancora schematico – indicano grandi salti di quota, di circa due piani, tra i singoli livelli. Ora è chiaro che su un lato le superfici sono delimitate da muri molto alti che digradano verso i due lati adiacenti. Da una parte questi spazi possono leggersi come cortili interni all'edificio o corti all'aperto, per così dire, mentre dall'altra si aprono alla vista sul paesaggio.

Scale e muro

Spostandosi da un livello all'altro, l'esperienza formale degli spazi, delle situazioni scenografiche, dipende da dove si guarda. Tuttavia, gli elementi che caratterizzano questo andamento non sono ancora